BUYING A HOUSE DEBT-FREE
EQUIPPING YOUR SON

By Steven and Teri Maxwell
Foreword by
Jim Bob Duggar

Buying a House Debt-Free

Copyright © 2014 by Titus2, Inc.

All rights reserved. Written permission must be secured from the publisher to use or reproduce any part of this book except for brief quotation in critical reviews or articles.

Ordering information:
Titus2, Inc.
1504 Santa Fe Street
Leavenworth, Kansas 66048
Phone: (913) 772-0392
Web site: Titus2.com

Published by:
Titus2, Inc.
Web site: Titus2.com

ACKNOWLEDGMENTS

Scripture taken from the HOLY BIBLE, KING JAMES VERSION.

ISBN 978-1-941183-00-7

Printed in the United States of America.

1

Nothing in this book shall be construed to be legal advice. Seek appropriate legal counsel as required.

This book was created in Pages. InDesign CS6 and Adobe Photoshop were used for layout and design.

Joseph Maxwell designed the cover and interior. Anna Maxwell implemented the design.

DEDICATION

This book is dedicated to the courageous young men who will say, "I can do this!"

TABLE OF CONTENTS

    Foreward 7
    Preface 9
1   Is It Possible? 11
2   Start Now 23
3   What's the Foundation? 37
4   Teach the Basics 51
5   Learning Difficult Lessons 65
6   Saving Versus Spending 81
7   Are Savings Robbers at Work? 99
8   What Skills Will He Have? 111
9   How to Acquire Necessary Skills ... 125
10 Is College the Answer? 139
11 Entrepreneur or Employee? 157
12 When the Moment Arrives! 171
13 The Cash Buyer 185
14 What If? 199
15 Live the Vision 215
    Resources 227

FOREWARD

For years, Michelle and I have used Steve and Teri Maxwell's resources on scheduling and chores to help our home run more smoothly and efficiently. The Maxwells speak to real needs in real families. I expected to find practical, motivating information in *Buying a House Debt-Free*, and I wasn't disappointed.

As a father of 19, I share Steve and Teri's desire to see young families living debt-free lives, even to the point of owning debt-free homes. In our book *Twenty and Counting*, Michelle and I tell our personal story of becoming debt-free.

Today many families are struggling under the weight of debt, and the economic times are uncertain. The stress they endure can destroy marriages and cause sleepless nights. To most being debt-free seems impossible and especially so regarding a house. However, in this book I read the inspiring stories of young men who have achieved the goal of owning a house debt-free. I would like that for my sons, and I think you would for your sons as well.

In *Buying a House Debt-Free* the Maxwells show us what a young man should do to save for a debt-free house. They talk about the necessary spiritual foundation and ongoing focus. They emphasize the importance of young men being productive with the years they have before marriage and the value of eliminating time and money robbers. They encourage young men to be entrepreneurs and savers. They even help us through the "what ifs" that might hinder us.

I haven't read a book before that tackled this subject for young men and gave convincing examples of success. I personally know two of the Maxwell boys who have purchased their homes debt-free, and I see in their lives what Steve and Teri are encouraging you for your sons. I believe this book could have a tremendous impact on the future of countless young men who will pursue the goal of owning a debt-free home. I think every family should read *Buying a House Debt-Free*, and I encourage you to catch the vision for your sons.

Jim Bob Duggar of TLC's *19 Kids and Counting*
Author of *The Duggars: Twenty and Counting*
and *A Love That Multiplies*

PREFACE

Three of our sons have purchased their homes debt-free with cash before they were married. As we write, our two younger sons are working toward that goal. It is not rocket science and certainly not impossible to achieve the goal of owning a home debt-free while still in one's 20s. Simply put, it is a way of life.

Some suppose that our sons had certain special advantages that enabled them to buy their homes debt-free and that not everyone has those advantages. Our sons had no special advantages or circumstances but only a vision set before them of hard work in their own businesses, denial of self-gratification, and a mindset for saving money. Plus, they experienced the blessing of the Lord.

We believe that most young men are capable of beginning married life owning their first home debt-free, and we believe that after reading *Buying a House Debt-Free* you will agree with us. We have seen that it isn't a matter of whether they will fail in this quest, but whether they will choose to go for it with a serious level of commitment. You will be encouraged as you see your sons rise to new purpose in life.

We will introduce you to young men who made the choices we hope your sons will make and now own debt-free homes. We are grateful to each of them for having the courage to go against the tide so they could purchase homes debt-free. These young men were willing to share their stories with us so that we could inspire you to foster those same goals for your sons. We have changed the names of all these young men (except for our sons) because some of them wanted to maintain their privacy.

We are thankful to the families who read a draft of *Buying a House Debt-Free* and gave us feedback. We are grateful to Jim Bob Duggar, Kevin Swanson, and Dr. S.M. Davis who took of their valuable time to read *Buying a House Debt-Free* and endorse it. In addition, our family members are our greatest critics and encouragers. They have also lived what we are challenging you to do.

We would like to see your sons owning homes debt-free when they walk the aisle and say, "I do." Will you join us in this exciting adventure?

1 IS IT POSSIBLE?

We want to introduce you to 26-year-old Ryan. He is a regular guy with an average income working as a firefighter, but he has certainly set himself apart. What's different about Ryan? He bought his home debt-free two years ago when he was only 24. Impossible, you say? Not at all, and we are here to convince you of that and, hopefully, to set you on the same trajectory for your sons.

In *Buying a House Debt-Free*, we will share the stories of young men who rose above their peers, young men who didn't have the average mindset, young men who didn't listen to those who would say a debt-free first home was nothing but a dream. Instead they believed buying a house debt-free was an achievable goal and determined to go for it.

Each of their stories is unique yet similar. There is an underlying fabric of faith, courage, and determination written in each life. All of these young men are just regular guys with regular abilities and regular ways of earning income, but they have turned their personal world upside down because they made choices that enabled them to own debt-free homes while still in their 20s.

Steve talked to these men personally to discover how they accomplished the feat of buying homes debt-free at such young ages. He came away from these interviews with awesome information. We hope the stories will inspire you to say, "If they can do it, my sons can do it, too!"

How Do Christians React?

We received a note from friends who wanted to relate a recent event to us. Their family had the opportunity to share music and testimonies about what the Lord was doing in their lives at a local church. When it was Mark's turn, the 14-year-old said he was saving to buy his house debt-free in the future. The audience erupted in laughter. Sadly, that was not the first time this had happened to the young man when he shared that part of his testimony.

We have a crisis. Have Christians so completely bought into the mortgage mindset of the world that they find a young man's goal of buying his first house debt-free ludicrously impossible and publicly laughable? Is not God at work in our lives, empowering us to be hardworking and creative in earning an income? Does not His Word say that the "borrower *is* servant to the lender"

(Proverbs 22:7), and does He not want us to be free? Didn't Paul pay not only his own way but others' as well by working hard at tent making? Have "we" so believed the various lies of the world that we think hard work and Christian ethics aren't rewarded?

Buying a House Debt-Free points to the power of choice and a loving, gracious God Who rewards hard work. "In all labour there is profit: but the talk of the lips *tendeth* only to penury" (Proverbs 14:23).

Next, this book should be an encouragement to everyone that we need not be slaves to a mortgage company. In Scripture, borrowing was a sign of a curse. "He shall lend to thee, and thou shalt not lend to him: he shall be the head, and thou shalt be the tail" (Deuteronomy 28:44). Are we proclaiming to a lost and dying world that we are blessed or under a curse?

We speak first to parents because you hold the keys in that you can set the direction for your sons' lives. You can guide and encourage them along the way.

Depending on their goals, young women may also profit from this information. The Proverbs 31 woman bought a field. "She considereth a field, and buyeth it: with the fruit of her hands she planteth a vineyard" (Proverbs 31:16). She was industrious with her time and resources. If this description fits a young woman, then she will benefit from this information as well.

Older adults with a job and family might come away with new ideas and hope, even though it will be more difficult for them than for a single young man. The longer one has traveled down a different road, and the more baggage he has accumulated en route, the more strenuous it is to reverse course.

This is not a *name-it, claim-it* book about pie-in-the-sky faith. Rather, it is about a practical faith empowered by God's grace that glorifies the Lord Jesus. It begins with a solid relationship with Christ that is growing and maturing. It moves into learning to listen to the voice and direction of the Savior. It culminates with the daily joy of walking faithfully with Jesus.

Much of *Buying a House Debt-Free* lays the foundation for becoming a small business owner or entrepreneur. Even if that is not your goal, the path presented can bring stability to your life.

Can Parents Give Their Children Houses?

You are probably like us. Though it is our desire to provide a debt-free house for each of our children, we are not financially able to do so. "House and riches *are* the inheritance of fathers …" (Proverbs 19:14). One thing we *can* do, however, is inspire them toward the goal of a debt-free home. We set that vision before them and help them own it. We educate them for a debt-free lifestyle. We equip them for it, and we are their greatest cheerleaders. We launch them down that road.

Some of you have young sons. Now is the time to begin showing them a better way. Others have older sons and may feel behind at this point. Be encouraged! As long as you are willing and your son is teachable, you can still achieve the goal. Whether your sons are toddlers, older teens, or somewhere in between, you will come to understand your important role in your son's buying his house debt-free.

You initiate the process by teaching your son that he will need to choose the debt-free road and then showing him how to walk it. It will take effort, determination, and just plain hard work on your son's part. You will be there as motivators and encouragers.

A Solid Start for Marriage

Think about how you would have benefited from having your house paid for when you were first married. Many couples struggle financially through those early years of marriage, which can result in added marital stress. Housing costs are typically the major expense families experience. Often a newly-married husband's income is not what it is 10 years later. Is that what you faced? Wouldn't you rejoice to be able to start your sons out with a much better beginning?

When we married, we didn't have the income or finances to purchase a home even with a mortgage. We began by renting, giving our housing money to another, without any residual benefit. After a few years, we took out a mortgage to purchase a home just as we did with all the subsequent homes we owned until we moved into our current house, which we built. Now we can say that it is delightful to know that the bank doesn't own our house. We were in our 50s and to achieve that outcome spent three years as a family building this house. What joy it brings to our hearts to be able to set our sons on a different path than the one we walked in our early marriage. We want to play a part in helping you experience that same joy by encouraging you to take action. Begin today with your children.

Think about this. How would you react if a young man called you interested in courting your daughter with the possibility of marriage and told you that he owned his home debt-free? Now consider the positive position owning a debt-free home puts your son in when he approaches a future father-in-law about his daughter. To a young woman's father, that house will likely represent some important aspects of the young man's character—character that the father knows could potentially facilitate a solid marriage for his daughter. It represents financial stability, which suggests that the father's daughter and grandchildren would enjoy a comfortable life. It may signal that your son is a young man the Lord is blessing and who has a measure of spiritual maturity.

Would it console you to know that, no matter what happens, your son, his wife, and your grandchildren would not be evicted from their home after missing a mortgage payment if he happened to lose his job in a worsening economy? Nearly all of us have known of families who have gone through foreclosure. It is an ugly process in which people—husbands and wives, parents and children—lose sleep, and marriages are often destroyed. What a blessing it would be if your children didn't have to face that sort of pressure. Will you purpose to help them toward the goal of buying their homes debt-free?

IS IT POSSIBLE?

Can you picture the financial stability if your son is self-employed and has no rent or mortgage to pay for his home each month? What can God do for His kingdom with the money your son is saving? How will that improve your son's current standard of living plus his financial future? What doors will be opened to your son because of his financial freedom?

It takes money to live, but this isn't just about money. Sons and daughters will learn that they can seek the Lord for direction and depend on Him for their needs. They will discover that they can trust the Lord no matter what comes their way. What is that worth?

Our Personal Experience

We want not only to motivate and inspire you for your children's future by sharing stories of young men who have achieved the goal but also to tell you from the parents' perspective what it feels like. We've joyfully experienced this because our three older sons have purchased their houses debt-free with cash at the ages of 24, 29, and 23, respectively. Our other two sons, who are 19 and 23, are working toward that same goal, and we are confident they'll reach it too.

We set the vision before them. We told them they could do it. We educated them as to why debt was a ball-and-chain attached to their ankles and why saving was important. We drew their hearts to owning the vision for themselves. We equipped them. We gave them the same keys to their futures that we are giving to you and encouraging you to give to your children. We are here as living proof that what others call impossible is indeed possible. It can be done by regular young men, with regular abilities, regular incomes, regular families, and regular parents.

Can you imagine the excitement in our hearts when a son comes home from the closing where he handed a cashier's check to the agent as payment not for the security deposit on an apartment but for payment in full for his own house? We celebrate! We clap our hands! We hug him, and he hugs us! We rejoice in the goodness of the Lord. Our son now has the fruit of the vision he embraced as a boy and of all the hard work he invested to achieve it. It took effort, but those years before marriage were used well preparing for the future.

We can tell you from personal experience that it is a wonderful feeling to walk through a newly-purchased debt-free home with our son. Talk about joy! "Prepare thy work without, and make it fit for thyself in the field; and afterwards build thine house" (Proverbs 24:27).

Seeking First

"But seek ye first the kingdom of God, and his righteousness; and all these things shall be added unto you" (Matthew 6:33). We want to encourage you to consider that freedom from debt is one of many desirable facets of a Christian's life. This verse admonishes us to seek God's kingdom first. In *Buying a House Debt-Free*, we emphasize what is necessary to achieve the goal of a debt-free house. Through that process, however, our primary desire is that our children are seeking the Lord Jesus.

If they don't know Jesus as Savior and are not experiencing His ongoing grace, grounded in daily personal Bible time, praying, engaged with family Bible time, enjoying serving others, they have a "heart" problem. In that case, they will likely need to do some spiritual work in their lives before they will reach their financial goals. We will also show you that financial stability can be one of the blessings God gives those who seek Him and obey His Word. We desire that our sons would first and primarily be soldiers of Christ. From that position, they advance not only spiritually but also in their careers and in saving for a home purchase.

Ryan's Story

We are going to tell you Ryan's story—the young man we mentioned at the beginning of this chapter. We want you to see how much Ryan is like your son and his family like your family. We want him to inspire you and your children.

When Ryan was 9, he had his heart set on a new ball glove, but he didn't have enough money to buy one. He went to his dad and asked for a loan. His dad wisely told Ryan to save his money and then go buy the glove. The initial debt-free seed planted in Ryan's life was that it is good to defer a purchase until you can pay for it with cash.

Later Ryan was contemplating buying his first vehicle. The spiffy newer trucks would require borrowing from the bank. The truck he could afford with his savings was certainly not as flashy as the one he could procure with a loan. As he thought about a loan and prayed about his purchase, he wondered what it would be like if he ever had trouble making a payment. Things happen, trucks break down, and repairs can be expensive. If he were making loan payments, he realized he might have a hard time paying for necessary repairs. Those thoughts were enough to convince him to purchase a vehicle within his budget with the cash he had. He had no regrets. That initial "cash only" seed his dad planted with the ball glove purchase received a nice shot of fertilizer.

Ryan worked at an automotive repair shop. With his steady income he decided to purchase a horse, which in turn taught him another valuable lesson. In addition to his main job, he began volunteering at a volunteer fire department. After a while, when he saw how little time he was spending with his horse and how much the horse was costing him, he sold the horse. He decided that from then on if he was going to have a hobby, it would be something that wouldn't cost him any money to support. He also decided that if he bought something, he would make sure he was able to sell it and get his money back when he was finished with it. He then learned an even greater lesson when he found that he was happier without so much "stuff."

The Debt-Free Home Goal

When Ryan was 14, he met a 24-year-old man who had purchased his house debt-free before he married. Ryan was intrigued, for he had never heard of anyone being able to do that. At 19, Ryan decided that if the other guy could buy a debt-free house, maybe he could too. So he committed himself to saving toward the goal.

Living at home without his parents charging room and board was a wonderful way to save money, and by the time he was 21 he had enough to start looking for a house. For a year and a half he waited, prayed, and continued to save. Finally, he found a house in foreclosure that appraised for $98,000 but just a few years earlier had sold for $103,000. It was 816 square feet, with two bedrooms and one bath. As he "watched" the house, in a few months the price dropped to $57,000. He placed a bid on it in a silent auction and prayed that if the Lord wanted him to have it, his bid would be accepted. He was able to buy his house for $51,000. He was 24 years old, and only five years had passed since he established his goal of buying his house debt-free.

The house isn't everything Ryan could want, but it's a fine starter house. He plans to invest minimally in making improvements and then look to upgrade. He's seen others who borrow because they want to have everything right away. Ryan said, "I am very grateful that God gave me the desire to live debt-free. It really does not take a lot of money when living a simpler life to stay within your means. God has been gracious in allowing me to have a steady job and be able to save without any major expenses coming up." Ryan is a wonderful example of hard work, a saving mentality, a goal to work for, not coveting, and patiently waiting on the Lord.

Catch the Vision

Frankly, our role as parents in this process is far easier than our sons'. We parents, however, first must commit that we will do all we can to help our children down this path. We play a huge part in our children's success. Will we decide that there is a better way than borrowing? It is an attainable goal worth pursuing. Will we do whatever we can do to help our children achieve this? Will you and your sons join the growing number who demonstrate, "I can do all things through Christ which strengtheneth me" (Philippians 4:13)? Most think it isn't possible for a young man to buy his house without a mortgage in this day and economy. They won't even make an attempt at it. We are going to show you that it is not only possible but also very exciting. The enthusiasm you're feeling is just the beginning. The real thrill comes when your son pays cash for his home. We have laid the steps out to make it as clear and simple as possible. Read this information and then read it with your sons. Own the vision in your heart and look forward to the day when your sons buy their houses debt-free!

Chapter 1 Questions

- Are you committed to help your son develop a vision to being debt-free?
- How would being debt-free have benefited your family?
- What goals have you set before your son?
- How would you rate your son's walk with the Lord on a scale of 1-10?

2 START NOW

The story of our oldest son, Nathan, officially begins at age 13. He and his younger brother, Christopher, age 11, approached us about beginning a lawn mowing business in our neighborhood. To that point, they had invested their free time in playing Little League baseball. As we grew concerned about negative influences in their lives and the way baseball was keeping us from daily family Bible time, we had encouraged them to set baseball aside. With sports out of the picture, they were interested in earning some money.

The plan was for them to rent the family mower and power trimmer until they could afford to purchase their own equipment. Finding customers didn't turn out to be difficult because they priced their work a little less than those who were mowing commercially. Their business got off to a great start. By the end of that first summer, they owned a new mower and weed eater.

A year later, we moved a mile away. That posed some challenges for them in serving their customers because it was a time-consuming, tedious walk with their equipment to mow yards in the old neighborhood. The solution was to build a cart they could pull behind a bicycle. They continued to do well, and they were each earning close to $20 an hour for their part-time work.

Not only were they making reasonable money for their savings, but they were also learning business skills. They enjoyed their work, and their savings began to mount. Nathan continued mowing lawns until he was 17.

The Next Step

At 17, Nathan moved into utilizing the computer skills he had learned during his high school years to earn income. Through his volunteer work formatting a newsletter for the homeschool group we led, he had become very proficient with WordPerfect. His WordPerfect skills were so advanced that those overseeing the WordPerfect online message board in which he participated asked him if he would be a SysOp. SysOps were volunteers who answered WordPerfect-related questions on the message board. Nathan was thrilled with this new challenge.

One day Nathan came to us and shared some discussions that the SysOps were having privately among themselves. We were concerned about the nature of these personal conversations, realizing the potentially negative influence these others could have on Nathan. After praying about it, we suggested Nathan resign from his SysOp position. That was a very difficult request for us and decision for him to make. He was learning a great deal and receiving much affirmation for his abilities. He thought computers were going to be his future, and stopping his SysOp job appeared to be the end of that vision for employment. After praying, however, he agreed to follow our lead and resign.

Soon after that, Sarah, our oldest daughter, spotted an ad in the free weekly-shopper newspaper. The computer store downtown was looking for someone to teach WordPerfect classes. Nathan decided it wouldn't hurt to apply. Steve drove him to the computer store because at 17, he did not yet have his driver's license. We encouraged our children to wait on driver's licenses until they had a need to drive and a steady income to pay for insurance. Up to that point, Nathan had the lawn mowing income but no real need to drive.

During the interview, Nathan learned that the position was to teach WordPerfect to the captains, majors, and lieutenant colonels from nearby Fort Leavenworth who took the store's classes. Since Nathan was young, the owner questioned his computer knowledge and abilities. Nathan pulled out his letter of recommendation on WordPerfect Corporation letterhead that he had received when he resigned as a WordPerfect SysOp. That cinched it. Nathan landed the job teaching WordPerfect classes for $25 an hour and got his driver's license right away.

Full-Time Employment

About a year or so after Nathan began teaching, the company Steve worked for needed someone to do short-term desktop computer support as a contractor for $25 an hour. Nathan put together a resume, and they hired him. Steve and Nathan began commuting together to the same employer each day. After the short-term contract ended, the company decided they would like to have Nathan continue doing computer work for them. Sometime later, the man who had hired Nathan went to work at Western Auto's data center in Kansas City, and to Nathan's surprise he called Nathan one day. He asked if Nathan would come to work for him at Western Auto. After prayer, Nathan moved to the job at the new location with a significant pay raise.

During this time, Nathan was living—rent free—in our home and saving money toward purchasing a home debt-free. With a steady job, good income, and few expenses, he was able to put the majority of his income into his savings account.

The House Offer

One October day the son of the widow who lived across the street came by our house to talk to Nathan. He told Nathan that his mom wasn't able to live alone any longer due to her poor health, and they were going to sell her house. He knew Nathan had expressed interest in the house and wondered if he would like to buy it. The man said they would have the house appraised, and Nathan would be able to have first opportunity of purchasing it. Nathan was delighted.

About a week later, the man came back saying the house had appraised for $88,000. Nathan said he was very interested in buying the house but would need to pray about it. The man was in no hurry, but he wanted it closed by early January. Nathan began to pray. There was one major problem: Nathan's savings account was around $10,000 less than the appraised value of the house.

After a couple of weeks of prayer, Nathan told us he felt the Lord leading him to purchase the house. He would tell the man he would buy it and trust the Lord to provide the extra money he needed.

About a week later, Nathan received an e-mail from a well-known publisher of technical manuals asking Nathan to write a 400-page book on Windows Operating System security for use by community college professors. This offer came about because of a Windows Operating System message board on which Nathan had been participating. The challenge was that they needed the book written in six weeks, and there were penalties if he didn't complete it on time. After praying, we all felt the Lord wanted him to write the book.

Nathan dove into his project, writing nights and Saturdays because he was still working at Western Auto during the day. He made great progress but wasn't quite done at the end of six weeks. They gave him a two-week extension, and he was able to finish the book. As you might expect, the book provided the extra money he needed to buy the house and to cover closing costs.

The very best part of Nathan's story is that he knew God's leading to say yes to buying the house even though he didn't have enough money and was committed to not borrowing. He heard the Lord give direction and had the confidence that if God said to do it, God would enable. Nathan saw how God provided through the book-writing project.

Setting the Goal

As parents, we can set goals for our children and communicate those goals to them. These goals can have a powerful influence shaping our children's lives. We would like to help you see the vital importance of giving your children a vision for living debt-free.

Starting in Nathan's early teen years, we began laying goals for our children before them, including being debt-free. Since we wanted them to know and understand those goals, we would discuss them with the children and explain why the goals were biblical and why they would be blessings in their lives. We wanted the goals to become something they owned for themselves. With our younger children, we learned that we could begin talking about the goals earlier in their lives and that they would gain much from watching their older siblings achieve those goals.

Because of the goal of debt-free living, our children began at young ages to strive toward that goal by saving what they earned and being frugal in what they spent. When Nathan needed a car to drive to Western Auto in downtown Kansas City, he had the money in the bank to buy an economical, reliable used car that could make the 70-mile round trip each day. Since Nathan had been saving for a house for years, when the widow's house across the street came up for sale, he was in a good position to buy it.

Our Personal Example

As we set before our children a biblical goal of being debt-free, we will want to challenge ourselves with it as well. Many of you reading this book are likely in debt, and that is perhaps one reason why you are drawn to a different way of life for your children. If we make excuses about why we need to borrow, we should expect our children to do the same. Instead, we can start now to work hard to pay off our debt. We explain to our children the bondage the debt has put us in and the joy we will have when it is gone. We can motivate them by admitting our failures and encouraging them to learn from those failures. Our personal example as parents is powerful in our children's lives. Jesus said, "Ye do the deeds of your father …" (John 8:41). As we live a debt-free life or work toward that, we will capitalize on giving our children a positive, debt-free role model to follow.

Mark's Determination

Remember Mark from chapter 1 who the church folks laughed at when he told them he was saving to buy a house debt-free? Most of us have experienced being laughed at. When a large group of people laughs at you, it will likely do one of two things. Either you will decide "that's enough!" and choose new "politically" acceptable goals or you will be all the more determined to stay on the path you are walking. Mark chose the latter. He is now a young man with even stronger determination.

How did Mark come to this commitment? He came to it through his parents' encouragement and the example of others. His parents shared with him about some bad financial decisions they had made and challenged Mark that there was a better way—being debt-free. He also observed how three young men purchased their homes debt-free, and he decided he could do it too. Don't ever underestimate the power of your example! Therefore, believing it to be attainable, Mark committed to the goal and began working toward it.

Starting Young

How does a young man like Mark or your son earn the sum of money needed to purchase a home debt-free? He starts! Nothing is accomplished unless the job is begun. Just like climbing a mountain, you have to take that first step, and then the next and the next.

Commitment is good, but without income one will never reach the goal. Let's look at Mark's example. When Mark's dad needs help in his piano business, Mark is able to work for him and earn income. Mark also recently bought a grand piano that needs repair. Over the next several months, he will restring and refinish the piano as time permits and then sell it for a profit. That is a double win. Mark will earn a reasonable wage for restoring the piano all the while he is becoming more skilled in his father's trade. That is like a school paying you to learn.

Mark took ITonRamp's Computer Essentials class (ITonRamp.com), splitting the cost of it with his parents. They wisely had him invest in the class knowing that when we invest in something, we are more likely to apply ourselves and value the investment. Plus it gave Mark the opportunity to learn to make wise decisions. Because he had to use some of his savings, Mark had to be sure it was something from which he believed he would gain significant financial benefit.

Since completing Computer Essentials, Mark has been purchasing computers on eBay, repairing them, and then selling them for a profit via eBay and Craigslist. He continues to learn more about computers and is gaining valuable skills through this business endeavor. Knowing how important the Internet can be to businesses, Mark successfully completed ITonRamp's HTML course. Now he is able to develop web sites he may need for his businesses or earn income developing sites for others. Mark has embraced the philosophy of being a lifelong learner. Next he is considering studying to get an electrician's license and do home inspections.

We appreciate knowing young men with vision like Mark. Their future is exciting because they are men who are willing to work hard and learn. At 14, Mark isn't making a lot of money, but he is focusing on it step by step, little by little.

We also deeply appreciate Mark's parents. They set the debt-free goal before him. They are behind him, encouraging him, and giving him counsel.

It takes a large sum of money to buy a house, and Mark has begun. It's just a matter of time before Mark will be standing in front of churches sharing his testimony to God's grace and power that enabled him to buy his house debt-free. We wonder if they will laugh then.

How to Remain Committed

Our family has taken great enjoyment in hiking together when we are able to go to Colorado on vacation. We love a challenge and have climbed a number of mountains that are over 14,000 feet—"fourteeners." We don't do anything dangerous, but we love a long day of hard exertion. The first one we climbed as a family was Mt. Elbert, the highest peak in the Rocky Mountains. The route we took was nine miles roundtrip with an elevation gain of 4,700 feet, and it took us 12 hours start to finish.

When you set a goal of climbing a fourteener, you need to be in relatively good shape, which requires weeks of preparation. Since we exercise six days a week, no special workouts are necessary, but for several months prior to our vacation we boost the distances we walk.

Having Scriptural goals for the children might be analogous to our daily workouts. They are the basis of conditioning that prepares us for the climb ahead. If someone doesn't own the goals, he might begin, but when the going gets challenging he won't continue because he isn't committed.

It's a long, slow (at least for us) climb, and it is all about making steady progress. Various challenges arise on the way, such as staying on the right path, or battling loose rock and windfalls, but life is filled with challenges so we keep moving toward our goal. It takes commitment and determination to stick it out and achieve the goal.

Climbing a fourteener is not all that difficult if one is in good condition and has proper supplies, such as lots of water, high energy food, and appropriate clothing. We have found that someone in marginal shape will likely want to quit when he becomes exhausted. The other family members are quick to provide encouragement that he can do it. He just needs to catch his breath and keep going. We would liken that encouragement to what parents can give to the son who is saving for a house. A host of things will come along and attempt to derail his saving efforts. Dad and Mom can be that voice of reason and encouragement to keep saving and not spending. The end is attainable. Will you be committed to helping him stay the course?

Who Is Wiser?

We are sometimes surprised at how often we hear parents asking their children what they want to be when they grow up. With this philosophy, a child with little life knowledge and not much spiritual maturity will, at his parents' request, base his future on his immediate whims and wants.

Could it be possible that your children would be better off in the years to come if, instead of asking them what they want to be, parents would give guidance toward biblical goals and vocations? If you begin to inspire your children toward being debt-free, they might, with your counsel, start a business that would become their future employment. Your children can have purpose and direction in their lives while they are still teens. They don't have to wait until they are adults.

Owning the Goal

Are you beginning to see how important dads and moms are for giving vision and direction to their sons and daughters? We have power to inspire, challenge, and motivate our children. It takes purpose on our part and the investment of our time and energy in their lives. Most of us can't give our children all that we would like to materially, but we can lay the biblical goal of being debt-free before them and then help them to embrace that goal for life.

Parents should know what is best for their children and therefore be the ones to give them direction. This is an important aspect of raising our children. We launch them in the right direction and then help them stay on course. We want to encourage you to begin today talking to your children about the importance of living debt-free and then setting in front of them a goal to own their homes debt-free. This is the first step toward your children owning debt-free homes.

Chapter 2 Questions

- What goals has your son embraced for himself?
- Is he committed to being debt-free?
- What has your son attempted that is difficult and greatly challenging?

3 WHAT'S THE FOUNDATION?

One day a couple who lived around the corner from us stopped by the house to talk with Christopher, our second son. They were retired schoolteachers whom we had known for many years. They came to tell Christopher that they had decided to build a new home and wanted him to know in case he was interested in buying their current house. Christopher had the finances for a house and began to pray and fast concerning that decision.

The house seemed perfect. Two schoolteachers without any children don't put much wear and tear on a home, and the husband had kept it up well. It was close to Nathan's house and reasonably priced.

When Christopher and Nathan had their lawn mowing business, Christopher faithfully saved his earnings. After high school graduation, he moved from mowing lawns to being self-employed under the umbrella of our family business doing website development, product photography, and assisting companies with accounting software, earning $25 an hour.

We have to confess that we felt the decision to buy the house was an easy one. Christopher had the money in savings and could write the $160,000 check. Yet, as Christopher prayed and fasted, he didn't have peace about buying the house. When the agreed upon time arrived, he said, "No."

Though we were a little disappointed with the decision, we were at peace. Christopher was a man. He had sought the Lord, and the Lord had said, "No."

A few years later, our family found itself in a crisis. We operated our Titus 2 ministry out of our basement with additional storage in the shed we had built for that purpose in the backyard. Even with the shed, we were out of room to store books. Commercial property seemed too expensive for us, so we wondered what the Lord would have us do. We were discussing this as a family one day.

Teri turned to Christopher and, being silly because it was so ludicrous, said, "You just need to buy our house, and then we could build a house with plenty of storage room on our property behind us."

To our shock, he said, "Honestly, I think I would be interested in that. I love this house."

With Christopher's affirmation, we began to explore the possibilities. We had purchased the one acre lot behind our house earlier. We had no plans to build on it but wanted it as a parking place for the large vehicle we anticipated for family ministry travel.

To build a house, we knew we would need to get a reasonable price for the family home, which meant that Christopher would not get a bargain. We decided to have our house appraised. Then we would proceed only if we thought we could build a home for the appraised value of the house and if Christopher thought the family home was worth that amount to him.

The appraised value of our house was $210,000. Christopher was satisfied with the price, and based on the building estimates and much sweat equity, we decided we could build with that cash.

Christopher was 29 when he closed on the house. It was exciting to see him sign the papers and have our family home become his. It was amazing to us that the Lord prevented him from buying the other house. All of this happened because Christopher had such a relationship with the Lord that he could petition Him for direction and then know clearly what the Lord's response was. The greatest foundation our children need as they begin their adult lives is an abiding relationship with Jesus Christ as Lord and Savior. Parents, this is critical for our children.

Seek Ye First

"Therefore take no thought, saying, What shall we eat? or, What shall we drink? or, Wherewithal shall we be clothed? (For after all these things do the Gentiles seek:) for your heavenly Father knoweth that ye have need of all these things. But seek ye first the kingdom of God, and his righteousness; and all these things shall be added unto you" (Matthew 6:31-33). A debt-free house doesn't start with a bank account; it starts with a spiritual account—seeking first the kingdom of God.

Seeking God's kingdom first is vitally important in our family and something that we emphasize much more than debt-free living. A result of putting the emphasis on our children's spirits is that we saw the impact it had on their ability to be debt-free. Being debt-free wasn't our motivation for fostering our children's discipleship, but it was certainly a wonderful outcome.

An entire book could be written on the spiritual aspects that are important for our children. Since that is not the goal of this book, however, we will simply highlight a few.

Is Your Child Saved?

The first necessary ingredient is salvation. Eternity is at stake, which is clearly much more important than finances and a house. Talk of salvation will be a common theme in a Christian home, and children often become interested in salvation around age five or six. They are old enough to be aware of their sin and to understand what they are hearing in church and at home about the gospel of Jesus Christ. Often parents experience the joy of being the ones to lead their children to Christ.

May we encourage you to make sure to sit down with your children who profess salvation and ask them, "Who is Jesus to you?" Do they give you religious answers such as, "He is God's Son. He is the Creator of the world. He is all God and all man. He is the Savior of the world"? Or do they give you relationship answers such as, "He is my God and my Savior. He is the One I live for. He is everything to me. He saved me from hell, and He is my Lord." The answers you receive should confirm the spiritual fruit you see in his life. If your child's salvation is questionable, please be earnestly praying for him and taking opportunities to speak to him of his sin and need of a Savior.

What's the Appetite?

Help your children develop an appetite for God's Word by teaching them to spend personal time in the Word every day. "As newborn babes, desire the sincere milk of the word, that ye may grow thereby: If so be ye have tasted that the Lord *is* gracious" (1 Peter 2:2-3). Peter used a baby's desire to drink milk as an indicator of a believer's spiritual health. A healthy baby wants—even demands—milk on a very regular basis. There is no quieting him when he is ready to be fed. Time in the Word is the spiritual nourishment your child needs to help him mature and become a man or woman who can make wise decisions.

For most of our family's history we ate the "Standard American Diet." On a steady diet of eating this nutritionally poor food, we had no appetite for nutritious food. Then when some health concerns arose, we eliminated the bad food and started eating healthy food. To our surprise, we quickly developed a taste and desire for food that was nutritious.

On the unhealthy diet, when presented with food that was good for us, we had no appetite for what our bodies needed. We've seen a similar issue in families with an appetite for spiritual junk food over spiritual nourishment. When families feed on things that are lacking spiritual nutrition, the children will have an appetite for that over God's Word. The flesh is the flesh, and we shouldn't be surprised by its power. The flesh is going to prefer entertainment over being fed from God's Word.

We would plead with you to evaluate your family. Why give your children appetites for things that will compete with God's Word? Such things will not only make time in the Word unappealing but will hinder your son's involvement in profitable endeavors such as serving the Lord and working to earn the money needed to buy his house debt-free. Instead, give him an appetite for being in the Word and nourishing his spirit.

Family Bible Time Discipleship

Another way to give children an appetite for the Word of God comes from family Bible time. Daily family Bible time has been a cherished part of our family's day for over 20 years. We have family Bible time in the evening as we gather together around God's Word in the comfort of our living room. We've discussed each other's day during the evening meal and will continue the conversation for a time once we move into the living room. Then we open our Bibles and spend the next 30 minutes or so reading and discussing God's Word.

During family Bible time we, as parents, have the opportunity to teach and disciple our children in the ways of the Lord through Scripture. We have found that, almost daily, we will read verses that apply to situations we are experiencing. Then we use that time to show the children through Scripture what God's view is on why it is important to be honest, diligent, responsible, debt-free, and so much more. This family time in the Word will be critical for building into your children's lives all that they will need to help them live debt-free.

We found this note in the returned manuscript from one of the families who read *Buying a House Debt-Free* before it was published. "We began nightly family devotion time shortly after being challenged by your family at one of your conferences about six years ago. We can't begin to tell you how it has changed our lives and family. Thank you!" If you don't have a habit of family Bible time, we encourage you to begin now.

Weekly Meetings

For close to 20 years Steve has been having individual meetings with each of the children every week. These meetings last anywhere from five minutes to a half hour depending on the particular needs. This is a special discipleship time with the children. When Christopher was getting married, he mentioned to Steve that he was really going to miss those meetings.

We found that before and after lunch on Sunday was a time for the meetings that enabled consistency for us. It took some effort to find a time slot that worked, but it was worth it.

During those meetings Steve asks the child if he has any problems with him or other members of the family. If so, they discuss possible solutions. He asks if there are things the child is hesitant to discuss but should. Steve is always evaluating the children's hearts and that to which their hearts are drawn. He has found these meetings to be invaluable in maintaining close fellowship with the children. Next to family Bible time, these meetings are key in discipling the children.

Hearts on Things Above?

Competition for your son's heart is likely a battle he must fight and win for his abiding life in Christ, not just for buying a house debt-free. He isn't going to seek first the kingdom of God if his heart isn't with God, and he certainly won't be saving his income. Men love to sky dive, jet ski, rock climb, hunt, fish, compete in sports, watch TV or movies, and a multitude of other things for a simple reason: They are entertaining, exciting, and get the adrenalin flowing. Unfortunately, they are usually quite costly, too.

The youth of previous generations seem not to have had as many enticing things to distract their heart focus from the Lord Jesus and from earning an income as in more recent years. So many fun and exciting things exist to consume time and money—sports and entertainment and even "techie" things that hook hearts and compete with Christ. Sadly, from what we have observed, the Lord often loses. That is why Paul admonished: "If ye then be risen with Christ, seek those things which are above, where Christ sitteth on the right hand of God. Set your affection on things above, not on things on the earth" (Colossians 3:1-2).

While we can see and experience the thrill of things on the earth, we cannot so readily see and experience the things of heaven. We believe that is why Paul prayed for those in Ephesus, "And to know the love of Christ, which passeth knowledge, that ye might be filled with all the fulness of God" (Ephesians 3:19). In reality heavenly things are more real than the things of earth because heavenly things will never pass away. Earthly things will all burn in time.

Parents, we should heed Paul's admonition and thereby set the example for our children. If earthly things have our own hearts, they have great power to draw our children's hearts as well. "… the lusts of your father ye will do" (John 8:44). Jesus was telling the Pharisees that they would follow after the lusts of their fathers. That is the way God designed us. Children are naturally drawn to the desires of their fathers. Do we as parents seek those things that are above, or do we pursue and yearn after the things of the earth? We can be our own worst enemies, but the good news is that for the sake of our children's future we can change.

Is the Kingdom of God the First Priority?

There can only be one first (or top) priority in our lives. The further down a priority is in the list from first place, the less likely it will happen. That is why Jesus told us what our first priority is to be. The Gentiles (world), He said, are consumed with food, clothing, and keeping the flesh happy, but Christians are to seek first the kingdom of God. "I love them that love me; and those that seek me early shall find me. Riches and honour *are* with me; *yea*, durable riches and righteousness. My fruit *is* better than gold, yea, than fine gold; and my revenue than choice silver. I lead in the way of righteousness, in the midst of the paths of judgment: That I may cause those that love me to inherit substance; and I will fill their treasures" (Proverbs 8:17-21).

A debt-free house is not the ultimate goal in life, but it can be a by-product of an abiding life in Christ. People often ask us what the "plan" is to buy a house debt-free. It is not a plan; it is a way of life. That is why this chapter is key. As we surrender our lives to Jesus and His purpose for our lives, a natural fruit is harvested.

We all have certain basic survival needs on this planet such as food, clothing, and shelter. In Matthew 6:31-33, Jesus is saying to let Him provide those things as we live a surrendered life. It is possible that the Lord may divert a son's savings away from a house purchase for His glory. He can do that with a surrendered life but not in a life in which the money has been squandered on the flesh.

Jesus said He will give us an abundant life. "… I am come that they might have life, and that they might have *it* more abundantly" (John 10:10). An abundant life is measured not by the things that we have but by our life in Christ. This is the example that we parents should live out before our children as we raise them. If our children observe our contentment in Christ, they should also welcome our goals for their lives.

The Power of Prayer and Fasting

The Lord has called us to be heavenly minded while we walk this earth in the flesh. Our weapons are not of the flesh but of the spirit. "For though we walk in the flesh, we do not war after the flesh: (For the weapons of our warfare *are* not carnal, but mighty through God to the pulling down of strong holds;) Casting down imaginations, and every high thing that exalteth itself against the knowledge of God, and bringing into captivity every thought to the obedience of Christ; And having in a readiness to revenge all disobedience, when your obedience is fulfilled" (2 Corinthians 10:3-6).

Our offensive weapons are the Word of God and prayer. "And take the helmet of salvation, and the sword of the Spirit, which is the word of God: Praying always with all prayer and supplication in the Spirit, and watching thereunto with all perseverance and supplication for all saints" (Ephesians 6:17-18). Prayer is a most valuable weapon and can become even more effective when it is undergirded with fasting. "And Jesus said unto them, Because of your unbelief: for verily I say unto you, If ye have faith as a grain of mustard seed, ye shall say unto this mountain, Remove hence to yonder place; and it shall remove; and nothing shall be impossible unto you. Howbeit this kind goeth not out but by prayer and fasting" (Matthew 17:20-21).

Jesus gave us the example of casting out demons and moving mountains accomplished through prayer and fasting. We have yet to meet someone who enjoys fasting, but we have found that fasting is a blessing and powerful. God used Christopher's fasting about whether to buy the first house he was offered to give him an answer in which he could place his confidence. As you face difficult decisions, make prayer and fasting a part of your life when you petition the God of creation. Teach your children to do the same.

Icing on the Cake

A little old house sat on the property where we eventually built our current house. Although the house was too small for our family, we thought we would use it as a guest house when visitors came to see us. One day when Steve was in the cellar, he noticed something odd about the stone foundation. He pulled a screwdriver from his pocket and gave the wall a little poke. To his surprise, the screwdriver easily penetrated the "stone" indicating that the house's foundation was crumbling. That old house was unfit for habitation and would eventually collapse because the foundation was crumbling.

A relationship in Christ is foundational to all of life, and if the relationship isn't good, the life built upon the foundation will be unstable and eventually crumble. Parents want the best for their children. Abiding in Christ and seeking first the kingdom of God will yield strong, stable lives for the glory of God. It begins with salvation and is then strengthened as we read His Word and seek first His kingdom. A debt-free house can be icing on a delicious cake. We will have a huge part in the success of our children. May we get them off to a good beginning.

Chapter 3 Questions

- What evidence do you see in your son's life that he is trusting Jesus as his Savior?
- Does he have a daily personal Bible time?
- How does he participate in family Bible time?
- Does he demonstrate a heart for spiritual things?
- Give some examples of times you fasted about something. What was the outcome?
- Give some examples of how the power of prayer has been demonstrated in your family's life.

4 TEACH THE BASICS

Right after homeschool graduation, 18-year-old Ben began working for a general contractor learning residential construction. That was the year Ben's relationship with Christ solidified, and Jesus became the passion of his heart. His boss was a hard man and difficult to work for. Therefore, Ben learned not only how to frame a house but developed patience and diligence as well. It was not a good environment for a Christian, though. While that sort of environment often deals a deathblow to a young man's struggling walk with Christ, in this case it turned out positively in Ben's life. Was the outcome good because Ben didn't work there long, because he and his dad discussed issues together, or because Ben was in the Word every day? We don't know the answer, but when the opportunity arose for him to work for a Christian general contractor, Ben was eager for the job.

Ben's dad was a good financial steward and made wise financial decisions. He was an excellent example for Ben. The home they lived in was purchased debt-free. It was old and not in good shape, but it was what his dad could afford to buy without borrowing after retiring from the military. The family worked together to make improvements, and, when finished, it was a fine family house. Ben wanted to have a debt-free home like his father.

At 23, Ben didn't have enough money saved to purchase a house, so he and his dad decided to build one together. The arrangement was that they would both invest cash and "sweat equity." They would keep track of how many hours each one worked on the house, and after they sold it, they would disperse the profit using a formula they had devised. First, each would be reimbursed for whatever cash he had provided. Then sweat equity would be calculated by multiplying the number of hours each man worked by an agreed-upon hourly rate. They even had different hourly rates for different types of work such as framing, electrical wiring, plumbing, and common labor. Then any remaining profit would be disbursed according to the percentage of cash each had invested. When they sold the house, Ben had increased his savings by a multiple of two and a half times!

With his debt-free house goal in mind, Ben purchased a city lot while he and his dad were building the first house. When that house sold, he had cash in hand to build the next house himself. He contracted the basement excavation and walls in October while he was waiting to begin building in spring. He did everything else himself except for the utility hook-ups and the refrigerant charge for the air conditioner. At 27, Ben now owns a new debt-free home that he built himself.

Building houses in the hours he wasn't working didn't give Ben much time for entertainment and spending money. Living at home with his parents without charge also cut his expenses greatly. His sweat equity gave him a much nicer debt-free home than he would have had otherwise. Because of some of those choices, Ben was able to do what most would say is impossible—own a debt-free home after only several years as a general construction worker.

Continued Learning

At one point, Ben realized that he had learned all he could while working for the Christian general contractor and that there wasn't much chance of advancement. After completing his house, Ben felt God's leading toward electrical contracting and began studying the electrical code. Not too long after that, at a pastor's retirement party, he recognized a homeschool friend he hadn't seen in years. The friend had begun an electrical contracting business and now had seven employees. He offered Ben a job, and Ben seized the opportunity.

Ben is an excellent example of someone committed to learning and growing. That's an attitude he saw in his dad. We would be surprised if there was anything his dad wouldn't try to do if there was a need, and we suspect Ben has the same "can do" attitude.

Notice how Ben's desire to learn electrical contracting skills was turned into action. So many "zone out" once they have a job. They are not seeking to learn and advance. Ben began aggressively studying the electrical code on his own even though he didn't have a job prospect. Then when an opportunity came along, Ben was prepared. He had some experience wiring his own house, and he had the necessary electrical knowledge because of his diligent study.

When God is leading in an area, our sons need to hear His direction and begin learning all they can, knowing that God will develop them further at the proper time. Ben obeyed the leading of the Spirit by studying the electrical code in preparation for a potential new job. Sadly, many are not accustomed to obediently responding to the Spirit's leading and miss great opportunities. May we help our sons become obedient to the promptings of the Lord.

Another chapter in Ben's life is that he has recently married. What a huge blessing it is to have their housing provided as he enters this new phase of life. God's timing is a beautiful thing.

Ben gives God the glory for his house. First, God used Ben's parents as examples for Ben. Then Ben had an obedient spirit and responded to God's leading. The fact that initially he didn't have enough in savings to purchase a home debt-free was not a problem. God showed Ben that the first step was to take his savings, join with his dad, and build a house. As parents, may our prayers express our earnest desire for all of our children to obey God however He leads.

What's Key?

In this section we will present several important characteristics that you will want to help develop in your sons to enable them to purchase their homes debt-free. We will limit our discussion to a few, even though we could discuss many more as they pertain to the goal of debt-free living.

Perhaps the most vital aspect is obedience to God. God gave man clear direction in the Garden. "And the LORD God commanded the man, saying, Of every tree of the garden thou mayest freely eat: But of the tree of the knowledge of good and evil, thou shalt not eat of it: for in the day that thou eatest thereof thou shalt surely die" (Genesis 2:16-17). Adam, like every human being who would follow, was the first to be given a choice. Would he obey, or would he disobey? Choice entered Scripture in Genesis 3, and it is shouted through the pages that follow.

Choice is the most powerful resource in your arsenal. God draws and empowers by His grace, but each has to make wise and obedient choices that please God. Most of Scripture is imploring people to make right choices. In addition, even if we choose the right thing, it won't do any good unless we obediently act upon that choice. Our sons can either choose to follow the God of creation or not.

A Two-Edged Sword

Do you remember the story of God's deliverance of Israel from bondage in Egypt to the Promised Land? God demonstrated His power to His people through mighty miracles—beginning with the plagues in Egypt, then crossing the Red Sea, next providing for them in the desert, and finally delivering Sihon and Og into their hands. They endured great challenges, but they always saw the Lord's faithfulness.

As they approached the Promised Land, God sent in 12 spies. Ten came back with a discouraging report while two said, "We can do it." Only Caleb and Joshua believed the Lord. They were ready to obey and go into the Promised Land and encouraged the people not to be fearful. God gave the nation of Israel a choice to follow Him in conquering the land of Canaan or to shrink from the task. Joshua and Caleb had hearts of faith that saw the opportunities while the others saw only the reasons it could not be done. Caleb and Joshua chose obedience and encouraged the rest to follow, but the nation chose to follow the naysayers.

Parents, we plead with you to decide right now. "Who" are you striving to raise? Wouldn't you love to raise "Calebs" and "Joshuas"? When the people murmured, Joshua and Caleb tore their clothes and said to the children of Israel, "…The land, which we passed through to search it, *is* an exceeding good land. If the LORD delight in us, then he will bring us into this land, and give it us; a land which floweth with milk and honey. Only rebel not ye against the LORD, neither fear ye the people of the land; for they *are* bread for us: their defence is departed from them, and the LORD *is* with us: fear them not" (Numbers 14:7-9). Do you want to help your sons receive the grace in their lives that comes when they choose to obey the Word? This grace helps keep them from sin, allows them to discern the Lord's voice, and gives them the qualities that will enable them to earn and save money for a debt-free house. Let's purpose to encourage our sons to obediently follow the Lord even though the flesh will cry out for the easy route.

An Extra Blessing Due to Obedience

God is so merciful and bountiful. When we obey Him, we can receive actual physical blessings in addition to spiritual ones. "And it shall come to pass, if thou shalt hearken diligently unto the voice of the LORD thy God, to observe *and* to do all his commandments which I command thee this day, that the LORD thy God will set thee on high above all nations of the earth: And all these blessings shall come on thee, and overtake thee, if thou shalt hearken unto the voice of the LORD thy God" (Deuteronomy 28:1-2). God promised to bless Israel with a long list of blessings when they obeyed Him. In verse five we read, "Blessed *shall be* thy basket and thy store." Their basket was their income, and their store was their savings. The Lord was saying that if the Israelites obeyed Him, He would bless their income and prevent things that would cost them their savings. We don't obey God so that He will bless us physically. Those blessings, however, are marvelous side-benefits of obeying Him.

Responsible

Our sons need to be responsible to fulfill their goal of debt-free lives. Otherwise it is just a fantasy. If they expect Dad, Mom, relatives, or the government to bail them out of financial difficulties, they are not responsible, and most likely will not end up with a debt-free house. Dictionary.com defines responsible "as answerable or accountable, as for something within one's power, control, or management." We are accountable to our Lord Jesus Christ for the choices we make in all areas of life. Two critical areas of personal responsibility that affect a debt-free home are time and money.

Our time is valuable, and we will spend it either wisely or foolishly. Money is also valuable, and we will spend it, too, either wisely or foolishly. A young man might have a goal of buying a house debt-free, but how he spends his time and money indicate how responsible he is in owning that goal.

Our children are responsible when they learn to use their time wisely by working. We would like for them to have a mind to work as did the people who were with Nehemiah. "So built we the wall; and all the wall was joined together unto the half thereof: for the people had a mind to work" (Nehemiah 4:6).

It likely took Noah 100 years or more to build the ark. Hour-by-hour, step-by-step, piece-by-piece with primitive tools—time and money—he worked, and eventually he finished. What if he hadn't finished before it started raining? What if he hurt himself and couldn't complete the project? There were plenty of reasons to quit the task. Regardless of all the "what ifs," though, Noah stayed with it until he accomplished the goal. He was responsible and committed.

That is why we teach our children to set themselves to the task at hand. "Who then is a faithful and wise servant, whom his lord hath made ruler over his household, to give them meat in due season? Blessed *is* that servant, whom his lord when he cometh shall find so doing" (Matthew 24:45-46). Noah put his hand to his work and built the ark as God commanded. The clock is ticking, and we cannot recover time wasted and money spent. Are we teaching our children to be responsible with their time and their finances?

Responsible young men will have goals, and the decisions they make will reflect those goals. As we saw earlier in this chapter, Ben was responsible. He owned the goal of a debt-free house and then spent his time and money in accordance with that goal. He started "now," first saving and then building. He was responsible in learning the electrical code when he felt God leading him to acquire new skills, and a new job followed soon after.

Diligent

Reading the stories of these young men who have purchased their homes debt-free reveals that the quality of diligence is evident in their lives. Each one grabbed opportunities he found. They weren't sitting around hanging out with their buddies but rather working at various endeavors.

We observe this diligence in Ben's life. He was not only willing to work a full-time job but also spent his evenings and weekends building a house to sell and then building his own home. He could have been using that time and money on fun entertainment, but if he had it is unlikely he would be bringing his new bride to a debt-free home made with his own hands.

As parents, you can direct your children to diligence as you help them learn to apply themselves to whatever task is at hand whether it is household chores, yard work, studying, or a home business. "For even when we were with you, this we commanded you, that if any would not work, neither should he eat. For we hear that there are some which walk among you disorderly, working not at all, but are busybodies. Now them that are such we command and exhort by our Lord Jesus Christ, that with quietness they work, and eat their own bread" (2 Thessalonians 3:10-12).

Be a diligent example to your children by being diligent yourself. Work alongside them so they can observe your attitudes. "Go to the ant, thou sluggard; consider her ways, and be wise: Which having no guide, overseer, or ruler, Provideth her meat in the summer, *and* gathereth her food in the harvest. How long wilt thou sleep, O sluggard? when wilt thou arise out of thy sleep? *Yet a little sleep, a little slumber, a little folding of the hands to sleep: So shall thy poverty come as one that travelleth, and thy want as an armed man*" (Proverbs 6:6-11).

Point out Scripture passages on diligence during family Bible time such as: "I went by the field of the slothful, and by the vineyard of the man void of understanding; And, lo, it was all grown over with thorns, *and* nettles had covered the face thereof, and the stone wall thereof was broken down. Then I saw, *and* considered *it* well: I looked upon *it, and* received instruction. Yet a little sleep, a little slumber, a little folding of the hands to sleep: So shall thy poverty come *as* one that travelleth; and thy want as an armed man" (Proverbs 24:30-34). If your family was to read these verses you could ask them:

"Does Scripture call the man wise?"

"How does Scripture describe the man?"

"Do you want those outcomes in your life?"

"How can you children avoid being poor?"

"What consequences do you see because of the man's laziness?"

To encourage your children, share that being diligent takes effort and that they need to purpose to be diligent, not slothful. When our children are diligent in the work God gives them, they set themselves apart from the rest. "The hand of the diligent shall bear rule: but the slothful shall be under tribute" (Proverbs 12:24). They will reap the rewards that accompany diligence and avoid the consequences inherent to laziness. "The slothful *man* roasteth not that which he took in hunting: but the substance of a diligent man *is* precious" (Proverbs 12:27). All this is part of the path to a debt-free house.

Patience and Contentment

People love instant gratification, and we expect "it" now! We see this both in our world and in Scripture. Let there be a one-second delay after the traffic light turns green, and there will be a cacophony of honking for the vehicle in front to get moving. As we drive through towns, billboards promote all the items we can own immediately with zero down and no payments for three months. *Don't have the money? Don't worry: You can still have your heart's desire.* Esau sold his birthright because he wanted food right away. Sarah wouldn't wait for children so she gave Hagar to Abraham to be his wife.

Our children need patience because saving for a debt-free home is a long-term goal. Obviously, it isn't going to be accomplished in a year or even two. If our children haven't learned to be patient, they will abandon the goal and spend their money for something that provides short-term enjoyment. Patience can be developed in small ways in the course of daily life and then applied to bigger goals such as buying a house.

To help our children learn patience, we can utilize not only normal parental teaching but also be role models for them. Do we immediately buy everything we want, or are we willing to patiently save and wait for it? Do we pray and do without until a future time? We can also use Scripture to illustrate patience and impatience.

Coming in right alongside of patience is contentment. "But godliness with contentment is great gain. For we brought nothing into *this* world, *and it is* certain we can carry nothing out. And having food and raiment let us be therewith content" (1 Timothy 6:6-8). If our children can be content with the most pressing needs of life, food and clothing, then they can be content with waiting to own a home debt-free. When our children are content with what they have, they will naturally not be spending money that they could save for a house. Covetousness and greed, which are the opposites of contentment, are our children's enemies as they strive toward the goal of a debt-free home. They will continually drain them of their resources. We can be examples of contentment for our children and then help them learn it as well.

The Naysayers

It's a guarantee we will face naysayers just as Joshua and Caleb did. Ten of the twelve spies thought the task was impossible, and rather than try it in the Lord's strength, they convinced the Israelites to quit. Naysayers give us volumes of reasons something won't work. Sadly naysayers can be like those 10 spies in discouraging us if we let them. Don't listen to them. Will we be with those who turn back and fall in the desert having missed the opportunity to proclaim God's enabling power? Or will we heed the positive voice of Caleb? "And Caleb stilled the people before Moses, and said, Let us go up at once, and possess it; for we are well able to overcome it" (Numbers 13:30). Caleb's confidence was in the Lord. We want you to face your naysayers one day with a son who holds a deed to a debt-free home, proclaiming God's enabling power.

The Qualities They Require

As your children make obedient choices, they will experience the power of God's grace in their lives. Personal responsibility propels your children toward success in their work and in other areas of their lives. Purchasing a home debt-free is a long-term goal. It takes patience, involving years and years of hard work. Living contentedly while pushing toward the goal will preserve the finances that are being set aside for the house rather than wastefully spending them on short-term desires of the flesh.

We believe that our children can develop these qualities. Our role as parents is to direct them toward what is important and away from what is not. We hold the keys in our hands that will first implant the goal in our children's hearts and then enable them to achieve that goal. Start today!

Chapter 4 Questions

- How has your son demonstrated obedience to the Lord's leading?
- What are examples of wise choices he has made?
- How he has been responsible with his time and money?
- What are examples of your son's irresponsibility?
- What are examples of your son's diligence?
- What are examples of your son's slothfulness?
- What are examples of your son's patience?
- What are examples of your son's contentment?
- What do you expect the naysayers in your life will say if they find out your son has a goal of a debt-free house?

5 LEARNING DIFFICULT LESSONS

James, a personal friend, shared his debt story with us hoping that it might help others avoid the trap in which he found himself ensnared. He was a happily married 25-year-old whose wife was pregnant with their fourth child. He and his family lived in a 2,500-square-foot, four-bedroom home on 3½ acres with a mortgage payment of roughly $1,300 a month. James had become a real estate agent to improve his family's income. That work looked so promising they decided he would quit his factory job and concentrate on selling houses full time.

James was not lazy. He (and the bank) owned five homes and was going to rent them out until he could sell them for a profit. Then the real estate market crashed, and, with it, James's commission-based income. Although James had never been late on a single payment in his life, he soon realized they were in financial trouble. He called the mortgage company, trying to be proactive, but they told him there was nothing they could do until his payment was actually late.

James and his wife knew they needed to sell their house so they made about $3,000 worth of improvements to make it more appealing than other houses in the slow-moving market. They used up their savings improving the house and meeting their mortgage payments. James had been very careful to buy houses that were marketable, but when the housing market crashed, houses were simply not selling quickly. Then, several months later, that dreaded moment arrived when they were late on their first payment, then another, and another.

They went into foreclosure on several rental houses while desperately trying to sell them. They finally sold two of the houses just before losing them to the bank. The family experienced tremendous emotional pressure as they were going through this time of financial hardship. James was working five part-time jobs to provide for his family in addition to meeting his financial obligations. Given his strenuous work schedule, he wasn't able to spend time with his growing family, and the stress mounted.

James and his wife were accustomed to God's blessing in every area of their lives. This new situation was foreign and unsettling. All of their previous projects had been profitable, but now, given the length of time it was taking to move houses and his long working hours, they were in trouble.

James admits his mindset was, "Lord, You have always blessed. Surely You will never let me be late with a payment."

Then after they were late for the first time, he thought, "Lord, You have always blessed. Surely You will never let us be 60 days late with a payment." Then they were.

"Lord, You have always blessed. Surely You will never let us be 90 days late with a payment." Then they were.

"Lord, You have always blessed. Surely You won't let us go into foreclosure." Then they did.

Finally, "Lord, You have always blessed. Surely You won't let us lose our home." Then they did.

Sadly, James's story is repeated in various lives across our nation. How can our sons avoid foreclosure and bankruptcy and all the stress and emotional trauma that go with them? It's simple. They can choose to live their lives debt-free. Without a mortgage, there is no foreclosure. Without debt, there is no bankruptcy.

Is Debt Good?

When we hear finances discussed, people generally endorse debt saying it is good as long as the debt payments can be made on time. Some "experts" even suggest being in debt. They indicate we could invest borrowed money hoping to make more on the money than we pay in interest. Actually, if someone has a mortgage, one of the best investments is paying it down earlier than scheduled. This is because the investment is certain rather than hopeful. The stock market, though, is hopeful rather than certain. That's because it regularly has corrections (i.e., loses 20% or more in value over five-year periods). People ignore the risk element of investing.

Others might also suggest that we use mortgage interest as a deduction on our income taxes to lower them. While this made sense to us early in our marriage, we began to hear some Christian financial teachers talk about being debt-free and a biblical basis for it. We started doing our own study and, before long, made a personal goal to get out of debt and not borrow in the future. It took us quite a few years to achieve that goal, but we haven't regretted it for a minute. Plus it has provided the basis for teaching our children about debt-free living and encouraging them to start their lives with that philosophy and thereby be far ahead of their parents financially much earlier.

Is Scripture Silent?

We would like to share with you a few of the Scriptures that cause us to want to be debt-free and to help our children become debt-free as well. We suppose the most intriguing aspect of debt found in Scripture is that the Lord used it to explain forgiveness of sin. Look at Matthew 18:21-23: "Then came Peter to him, and said, Lord, how oft shall my brother sin against me, and I forgive him? till seven times? Jesus saith unto him, I say not unto thee, Until seven times: but, Until seventy times seven. Therefore is the kingdom of heaven likened unto a certain king, which would take account of his servants."

Jesus uses "therefore" to point back to forgiveness of sin and draw His listeners to an analogy. The Lord then tells the following story about debt as an easy-to-understand example to explain how sin is undesirable and needs to be resolved.

"And when he had begun to reckon, one was brought unto him, which owed him ten thousand talents. But forasmuch as he had not to pay, his lord commanded him to be sold, and his wife, and children, and all that he had, and payment to be made. The servant therefore fell down, and worshipped him, saying, Lord, have patience with me, and I will pay thee all. Then the lord of that servant was moved with compassion, and loosed him, and forgave him the debt. But the same servant went out, and found one of his fellowservants, which owed him an hundred pence: and he laid hands on him, and took *him* by the throat, saying, Pay me that thou owest. And his fellowservant fell down at his feet, and besought him, saying, Have patience with me, and I will pay thee all. And he would not: but went and cast him into prison, till he should pay the debt. So when his fellowservants saw what was done, they were very sorry, and came and told unto their lord all that was done. Then his lord, after that he had called him, said unto him, O thou wicked servant, I forgave thee all that debt, because thou desiredst me: Shouldest not thou also have had compassion on thy fellowservant, even as I had pity on thee? And his lord was wroth, and delivered him to the tormentors, till he should pay all that was due unto him. So likewise shall my heavenly Father do also unto you, if ye from your hearts forgive not every one his brother their trespasses" (Matthew 18:24-35).

Let's see what lessons we can harvest from the Lord's example using debt. We have listed some. Can you add to them?

1. There comes a time when payment is due. If the funds aren't available, it can mean disaster for the family.

2. Whether a large or small amount is owed, serious consequences can follow.

3. When borrowing, one presumes that conditions will be favorable to repay in the future.

4. The borrower places himself under the power of the lender. "The rich ruleth over the poor, and the borrower *is* servant to the lender" (Proverbs 22:7).

5. The debt would have weighed heavily on the borrower, who knew the potential consequences should he fail to pay.

6. _____

7. _____

Another Debt Example

In Luke 7:36-40, the Pharisees criticize Jesus for allowing a sinful woman to wash His feet with her tears and hair. In Luke 7:41-42, Jesus responds with another example using debt. "There was a certain creditor which had two debtors: the one owed five hundred pence, and the other fifty. And when they had nothing to pay, he frankly forgave them both. Tell me therefore, which of them will love him most?"

Jesus is explaining that there is relief and gratitude when the debt is paid in full. The greater the debt, the greater the gratitude because of the relief from the weight one has felt due to the debt load. Sam Walton, founder of Walmart and one of the richest Americans who ever lived, said that not a day went by when he didn't feel the weight of his personal debt. Living without the pressure of debt is a wonderful thing.

The Greatest Debt

What is the greatest debt man owes? Isn't it his sin debt to God? No one would say that our debt of sin is desirable because as long as we owe it, we are headed for hell. We want to have that account settled. Jesus is the payment for our sin. He hung on the cross and uttered His last words "It is finished" (John 19:30). The account was then paid in full for those who would receive Jesus as their Savior. The Father is satisfied with His Son's being offered as payment for our debt of sin. "And you, being dead in your sins and the uncircumcision of your flesh, hath he quickened together with him, having forgiven you all trespasses; Blotting out the handwriting of ordinances that was against us, which was contrary to us, and took it out of the way, nailing it to his cross" (Colossians 2:13-14).

Presuming or Waiting

"Owe no man any thing, but to love one another: for he that loveth another hath fulfilled the law" (Romans 13:8). That is pretty clear. We've heard some explain that this verse means not to owe someone a debt you can't repay. "If you are making the agreed-upon payments," they say, "then the lender is happy, and you are happy." But how does one know that he will always be able to make the payments?

One of the biggest problems with borrowing is that we must presume upon the future. To promise we will repay something in the future assumes we know what the future holds for us and that we will have the money in the future. "Go to now, ye that say, To day or to morrow we will go into such a city, and continue there a year, and buy and sell, and get gain: Whereas ye know not what *shall be* on the morrow. For what *is* your life? It is even a vapour, that appeareth for a little time, and then vanisheth away. For that ye *ought* to say, If the Lord will, we shall live, and do this, or that" (James 4:13-15). Sadly, we've never seen a loan contract that says, "I promise to pay if the Lord wills." When we sign, we are giving our word that we will repay the money according to the agreed-upon terms regardless of what occurs in the future.

Things happen, and the best of plans fail. People borrow and then can't repay. Scripture calls that person not unfortunate, nor unlucky, but wicked. "The wicked borroweth, and payeth not again: but the righteous sheweth mercy, and giveth" (Psalms 37:21).

Is it possible that the fact that God has not provided for something we want is His way of indicating it isn't for us at this time? If we borrow to gain access to material possessions, that may be an indication that we are not willing to be content and wait on God's timing and provision in our lives. "And having food and raiment let us be therewith content" (1 Timothy 6:8). These are valuable lessons to teach our children. If God wants us to have it, He can provide for it.

It would make it much simpler if the Lord said to us, "Thou shalt not borrow." That is very clear and easy to understand. The Lord did not say that, though, and we must be careful not to make commandments when the Lord hasn't made them. When we look at the previous verses, we see that at best Scripture presents borrowing as unwise due to high risks, presuming on the future, not being content, and the appearance of the lack of God's blessing on the person's life. We need to train our sons to seek God's best in every area of their lives. If they are desiring God's best, we don't believe that borrowing plays a part in their lives.

Is There a Hidden Hook?

There is a tool rental shop in our hometown of Leavenworth, Kansas. One thing about renting from our local shop is that they are very expensive compared to the rental stores in Kansas City. Steve asked the manager why their rates were so high, and the man said, "Hey, we are the only one in town." When you go to someone who has something you need, he can charge what he feels he can get for it. Sometimes that is called "whatever the market will bear."

That is the way it is with borrowing. You go to someone who has something you want and for which you are willing to pay. In this case, it is money. The one who is asking for the money must be willing to pay for the privilege of using the other person's money. We know that is called interest. The one with the money is able to charge whatever interest the market will bear or the legal limit. Normally interest steeply increases the total amount we pay for an item.

Deuteronomy 28:12 says the sign of someone blessed by the Lord is that, "The LORD shall open unto thee his good treasure, the heaven to give the rain unto thy land in his season, and to bless all the work of thine hand: and thou shalt lend unto many nations, and thou shalt not borrow."

If we don't have the money for something we wish to purchase, and decide to borrow, we should expect the total amount we will pay to be considerably more than if we had the money ourselves. We have to compensate the one who is letting us use his money, and he sets the price and terms. "He shall lend to thee, and thou shalt not lend to him: he shall be the head, and thou shalt be the tail" (Deuteronomy 28:44). We don't want our children to be the tail.

How Much Will It Cost?

To bring some reality to our discussion of debt in purchasing a house, let's work our way through an example that would involve your son getting a loan for $150,000 to purchase a house.

> Loan amount: $150,000
> Term: 30 years
> Interest: 4.5%
> Private Mortgage Insurance: $123
> Payment*: $883
> Total Paid: $273,609
> Interest Paid: $123,609
> http://www.zillow.com/mortgage-calculator/
>
> *No property taxes and homeowner's insurance are included in payment because a debt-free house would have those as well.*

Just looking at the amount of interest that will be paid over the course of that 30-year mortgage is shocking in itself. Interest of 4.5% sounds pretty good, but when your son notices that the interest over the lifetime of the loan is almost equal to the price of the house, that's a whole different picture.

That 30-year loan term is enough time for your grandchildren to be born, grow up, marry, AND for several great-grandchildren to be born. This loan is a *l o n g* commitment. Might unforeseen financial events happen in your son's life during those years? We have seen very troubling economic times recently. What lies ahead?

If your single son earned $52,000 a year with an hourly rate of $25, he would make $1,000 a week and take home $722 (in 2013 in Kansas, approximately). If he gave a tithe of $100, he would be left with $622 of spendable income per week.

Then, let's say property tax is $1,200 a year and homeowner's insurance is $600. That will be another $150 a month added to the house payment. This means, not including maintenance, his house costs are consuming 41% of his monthly spendable income. Don't forget what it costs to pay back borrowed money. For every dollar you want to spend, you will have to earn about $1.50 for income tax, Social Security, Medicare, and tithe that will come off first.

If your son's house is debt-free, however, his monthly housing expenses for taxes and insurance are 6% of his monthly spendable income. Which do you think your son would prefer to pay for his housing each month, $1,033 or $150? We know which we would choose!

Comparison between mortgage and debt-free home		
Spendable Income	$2,488/month	$2,488/month
Pay on House	$1,033	$150
% of Spendable Income	41%	6%

The Great Tax Write-Off Myth

We remember when we first began to consider being debt-free. As we shared that vision of our heart with others, they quickly told us we wouldn't be good stewards of our money if we didn't have a mortgage. They wanted to convince us that a mortgage is a stellar tax deduction and, therefore, a wise decision. We ran the numbers, and here is what we discovered.

For that $150,000 home loan in the previous example, the first year of the mortgage the interest is $6,701 (zillow.com/mortgage-calculator), and only $2,420 in principal comes off the loan amount. Using Intuit's online tax estimator, we learn that by paying $6,701 in interest, one saves a whopping $457 in Federal income tax.

> Federal tax with no interest deduction $3,911
> Federal tax with interest deduction of -$3,454
> Estimated tax savings due to interest   =$457

Also keep in mind that these calculations are for the first year of the mortgage. That is when the tax deduction is the best. Each year, as the portion of the interest goes down, so will his refund. To help him better understand, you could offer to give your son a $457 "present" at the end of the year *if* he will pay you $883 ($10,596/12 interest and PMI) each month. Frankly, we would prefer to pocket the $10,596 and pay the additional $457 in taxes. What about you? What about your son?

Can Borrowing Damage a Marriage?

Newlyweds often struggle with finances as they are beginning life together and setting up a household with a low-income level. There are enough challenges in a marriage without adding financial tension to it. A *New York Times* article titled "Money Fights Predict Divorce Rates" (December 7, 2009) reveals just how serious money problems are in marriage. The article reports on a study by Jeffrey Dew of Utah State University that found that couples who disagree about finances less than once a month were over 30% less likely to get divorced than couples who reported disagreeing about finances a few times a month.

We have heard a saying that a parent will never be happier than his least happy child. A divorced child is surely a recipe for sadness. Don't we want to do everything we can to give our children the right start in life? Children who have the lifelong goal of living debt-free and waiting on the Lord to provide will likely experience far less financial stress in their lives.

Remember Jesus' example in Luke 7:41-42 of those who were forgiven of their debt? That pressure was gone. The more debt they were forgiven, the greater their gratitude. Why not do everything you can to set your sons on the path of a debt-free life? They will be so grateful to you just as Ben is to his dad for setting the debt-free example and teaching him to have the same goal.

Will He Be Able to Resist?

Debt is still seen as normal and, for many in our society, even necessary. It is likely that well-meaning friends or extended family will encourage your children to borrow. You can inoculate them against debt-fever by equipping them with solid Scriptural reasons plus the black-and-white logic against debt.

Jesus used debt in relation to sin for a reason. People understand the burden they have when they are under debt. Jesus wanted them also to be able to feel the heavy weight of sin in a practical way so they would be determined to be free of sin.

We need to help our children see debt as something to avoid. They should understand how expensive it is to borrow. We can help open their eyes to the financial benefit of paying *no* interest. They will be much further ahead to pay cash for a house without all the interest charged in a mortgage. The pittance they would save on the interest deduction of their income tax is overshadowed by the large amount of interest they would pay. They should be able to see how debt can be a ball-and-chain to a marriage. It is a burden that they can avoid.

We are delighted to watch our sons move through their lives without the many grave problems debt brings. Each of the debt-free young men in this book has made stellar financial choices that are producing good fruit in their lives that goes beyond a bank account.

Chapter 5 Questions

- Before reading this book what were your views on debt?
- How does Scripture present debt?
- What is the greatest debt that man owes?
- What problems does debt bring?
- How is borrowing presumption?
- Which would you prefer—no mortgage payments or the tax savings due to having claimed mortgage interest?

6 SAVING VERSUS SPENDING

Bill, a homeschooled young man, purchased his two-bedroom, one-bath, 1,140 square-foot-house on 1½ acres just after turning 20. His story is unique and illustrates that a debt-free home is within grasp even at a very modest income level.

At 15, Bill's parents thought it would be good for him to learn to work outside the home. He got a job at a gas station working for a man who was not an easy boss. Bill feels God used his employer to teach him the powerful lesson of submitting to authority, especially when the authority is difficult. He worked at the gas station four years earning minimum wage but saving all he could.

When Bill was 19, he dedicated his life to the Lord and became serious about Christ. He spent two months helping a missionary with a vacation Bible school in Alaska. After coming home, he applied for a job at a local manufacturing company with 5,000 employees. He was hired for $8.50 an hour and worked 40–50 hours a week as a temporary employee.

Soon after, Bill found a foreclosed house for sale. It appraised at $76,000, but because the previous owners had removed the bathtub during a remodeling project and hadn't installed a new one, the house could not be sold to anyone requiring a loan. It was technically uninhabitable and would have to be a cash sale.

Bill ended up paying $16,600 for it. He hadn't saved quite that much so his parents loaned him the small additional amount needed. Since buying the house, Bill has been hired as a full-time employee and now earns roughly $12 an hour. One year after purchasing the house, he has almost paid off his parents.

Was It Luck?

Was this just a "lucky" break for Bill? As Christians, we know that there is no such thing as luck. We look to the hand of a loving, mighty God Who desires to reward those who diligently seek Him.

Bill is a hardworking young man with initiative and the desire to raise a family that will honor and glorify the Lord. Bill has applied for a better job at his company. His company offers many courses to their employees on a wide variety of job-related topics. He has taken some courses that qualify him to "bid" on a better-paying job of $20 an hour. Bill said he is waiting on the

Lord. If the Lord wants him to have it, he will get it. If not, he will apply again later.

One might think that most of the employees would take advantage of classes the company offers for the chance to improve themselves and secure a better job. Bill said that most do not, however, because "they seem to be satisfied just to draw their pay for 40 hours a week."

Bill wants to please God in all that he does. He isn't satisfied with coasting along. He desires to learn and advance. He is an example of the power of right choice.

We asked Bill why he was still living in his parents' home when he had his own house. We have been asked that question, too, many times because each of our sons lived with us prior to marriage even after purchasing his house. Bill said, "My house isn't quite finished yet, for one thing, and I can also save a lot of money by living at home. When I don't live in my house, the utilities are lower, and I don't have to pay for food. I also don't subject myself to much of the temptation with which single people living alone have to deal."

Lessons from Bill

If one is going to borrow from someone, borrowing from one's parents is best because he is borrowing against his inheritance. "A good *man* leaveth an inheritance to his children's children: and the wealth of the sinner *is* laid up for the just" (Proverbs

13:22). Also having his parents paid back quickly is a testimony to how careful Bill has been not to spend his money.

Bill's focus is not first on making money but on seeking and serving the Lord Jesus. "But seek ye first the kingdom of God, and his righteousness; and all these things shall be added unto you" (Matthew 6:33).

Bill had to be an extremely frugal young man, saving every penny he possibly could. The fact that Bill was able to purchase a house appraised at $76,000 on such a limited income should be great encouragement to others who don't have big paychecks. Bill is a testimony that one can be faithful in little, and God will add to it. "And that ye study to be quiet, and to do your own business, and to work with your own hands, as we commanded you; That ye may walk honestly toward them that are without, and *that* ye may have lack of nothing" (1 Thessalonians 4:11-12).

Will He Spend or Save?

In *Preparing Sons to Provide for a Single-Income Family*, we shared the formula "income must exceed spending." We will expand that formula and state it now as *"income minus spending is the maximum a person can save."* Regardless of the size of one's income, the amount someone spends will have direct impact on how much he can save. The more one spends, the more he must earn to save. The more he spends, the less he saves.

We found an article dated 2/21/12 on Forbes.com reporting that the basketball star Allen Iverson earned over $200 million in his NBA career, and now he's reported to be broke. Most of us can't imagine earning roughly $12.5 million a year over a 16-year span. The article describes the problem, which was not insufficient income but unlimited spending. Often, when someone incurs financial problems, he immediately thinks of ways to bring in more money. But one should look at spending first to balance the budget. One has to cut spending to where it is in line with the budget and long-term goals. Emphasize to your son how critical it is that he minimize spending if he wants to achieve his savings goal. Bill is the proof that even with a small income, savings will increase if there is little spending.

Will He Maximize Saving and Minimize Spending?

In chapter 4, we shared several character qualities that are key if your son is to buy his house debt-free. We mentioned being responsible, diligent, patient, and content. Perhaps another quality we could add to the list would be frugal. Think about Bill's income. If he hadn't been ultra-frugal with his spending, he wouldn't have been able to save for his house.

The following table illustrates the effects of various spending levels on a savings goal of $100,000 versus different hourly rates of income. We can see how meticulously careful someone making a low hourly wage should be to spend very little. It also shows, however, that it is very possible for someone with less income to save $100,000 in under nine years. We find the data very encouraging. If a son began saving when he was 18, by the time he was 27, he would have a reasonable house in many areas of the country. The following numbers are calculated after taking out tithe and tax, based on working 40 hours per week.

Number of Years to Save $100,000						
Weekly spending	$10/hr	$15/hr	$20/hr	$25/hr	$40/hr	$50/hr
$50	8.6	5.4	4.1	3.4	2.2	1.8
$100	11.1	6.3	4.6	3.7	2.3	1.9
$150	15.6	7.5	5.3	4.1	2.5	1.9
$200	26.3	9.3	6.1	4.6	2.6	2.1

We can observe that saving $100,000 while earning $10 an hour is attainable in 8.6 years when spending $50 per week. Above that spending level, purchasing a house at that price is more of a dream. The young man should make a concerted effort to get income up while keeping spending down. If a house could be found for $50,000, however, the saving time is now only four years. That is achievable.

Will He Wait on the Lord?

We had a couple of adult missionary children spend the night at our home on their way to the East Coast. Their car was packed full of clothes they had been given. They were raised to look to the Lord to provide for their needs, and they didn't buy things hastily. "But my God shall supply all your need according to his riches in glory by Christ Jesus" (Philippians 4:19). They shared how exciting it was to see the Lord meet their needs, yielding the fruit of patience and contentment as they looked to Him. God gets the glory.

Through the years our family has tried to avoid purchasing things that are not true needs. A host of gadgets are cool to have and yet easily done without. The other day, Steve was tempted to get a small, handy car vacuum when he saw one in a sales flyer. But we have a Shop Vac that works just fine. It means that we take the vac down from the wall and carry it to the car, but we don't have to spend money to buy a new car vacuum.

We will bless our children if we teach them to consider whether a purchase is a need or a want. Then if it is a need, we can direct them to pray for the Lord to provide. He might provide the item itself or the funds to purchase it. Contentment and frugality combine to help our sons make significant headway toward saving for a house.

Can He Do It Himself?

If we can instill in our children a do-it-yourself mentality, they will save a considerable amount of money over the years. With our taxes plus tithing, remember that $1.00 saved is equivalent to $1.25 to $1.50 earned (depending on your tax bracket and giving).

An expensive expert can fix or maintain many things on a car or around the house easily, but we can learn to do some of these tasks ourselves. Steve finds changing the car oil a hassle. Locating everything he needs, buying the oil and filter, changing the oil, and then disposing of the old oil—all takes time. Driving in to the local "fast lube" and waiting for the oil change to be done requires about the same amount of time but costs at least twice as much. It wouldn't be difficult to save over $5,000 throughout a lifetime if one is willing to change the oil himself.

We used to pay a company to apply all the right chemicals to our lawn at the proper times. When we found that the yard didn't look all that great, however, we figured out the costs of self lawn maintenance and realized we could do it much less expensively. When we did so, the yard looked better than it had with the lawn service, and we saved a significant amount of money each year. Yes, maintenance and upkeep takes time, but it is worth it.

We have worked as we raised our children to have them learn the "do-it-yourself" mentality by including them in the projects we are doing. When the oil needed to be changed, and we had a son the right age, he was helping Steve. When the girls were old enough to learn to sew, Teri was teaching them.

If our children learn to do it themselves, they won't have to pay someone else and they learn valuable lessons. First, they learn to be frugal. They also learn how to maintain what they own. Maybe another lesson is that the more we buy, the more things we have to maintain. There are many solid reasons to teach our children to think twice before buying.

Can Anyone Beat Living at Home?

It takes money to live. That is a reality our children will learn as they begin to experience the world. When they are saving their money, they will discover that their parents' home is the most inexpensive place they could live.

We decided we didn't want our children to pay to live with us. "A good *man* leaveth an inheritance to his children's children …" (Proverbs 13:22). This verse indicates that we are to prepare our children financially for life. One of the ways we can do that is by helping them acquire a house that is paid for. Allowing them to live at home while they save their money will let them achieve their savings goal all the sooner. We suggest that you look again at the table earlier in this chapter that shows how spending impacts savings. The best bonus of our children living at home until they are married is that we get to enjoy them all the longer. We treasure those years.

Saving for a Need

About 20 years ago, we had a leak in our roof over the garage. The entire roof was old and hail damaged and thus needed to be replaced. We didn't have the money for a new roof, and that leak troubled Steve greatly. He was ready to get a loan and be done with it.

Teri wondered about patching the leaky area while saving for the new roof. Steve knew he could patch it, but it would be ugly and only temporary. He reluctantly agreed to try it, though. He patched the roof, and we began saving. Our memory is that it only took about a year of saving before we had the funds for a new roof. Through that time, God faithfully provided in exciting ways while we saved.

Another time, prior to the leaky roof, we had a major need. Steve was driving 45 minutes each way to work. His car was ancient and had high mileage. He became concerned about missing work due to car difficulties. Steve was inclined to borrow for another car, but Teri was again the voice of reason and suggested we try saving while the car was still running. Steve's flesh lost the battle with his spirit because he knew that was the better approach. We saved everything we could and eventually we had enough money to purchase a new economy car. We also had the joy of working as a family toward a financial goal and the blessing of watching the Lord provide through our combined frugality in unexpected ways.

A Savings Goal

We suggest you work with your son to set a long-term savings goal plus short-term yearly goals. For our sons, the goal was $100,000 because a modest starter home in an acceptable neighborhood could be purchased for that amount. Because Christopher was 29 when he bought his house, he had over $200,000 available.

When your son begins to earn a steady income, help him set yearly goals that will allow him to achieve the final goal by a desired age. This will give him a feeling of accomplishment when he makes the goal and motivate him if he isn't hitting it.

Setting the goal of a debt-free house in front of our sons means that when they put money toward it, they can see progress, and they know they are working toward a specific outcome. The goal helps them remain willing to defer current spending and to make frugal choices.

What Is The Best Way to Save?

We wish we knew where best to save. Our family has used banks and savings and loans. Although the interest today is pitiful, at least it is FDIC insured. Investing in the stock market can be risky. We are told that the time frame that one would be saving for a house is too short for stock market investing, which should normally be 20 years or more to ride out financial storms and corrections.

Our approach has been very conservative considering the goal and how difficult money is to earn. Also, many investments are essentially buying a portion of a company, and we wouldn't have peace about being a partner with certain companies.

Some suggest buying real estate as a way to protect and grow their money. Remember James's story and how the real estate market collapsed? When the real estate market collapses, houses lose value and those with mortgages owe more than their house is worth. Plus, it still takes a large amount of cash to buy real estate without going into debt.

Some suggest purchasing gold and silver, but there can be significant swings in their value. We think those who are in the business of buying and selling it for commission are the ones who do best with it.

For us, the bank was solid and as secure as the world's money system can be. Each one will have to seek the Lord before making a decision.

Giving

God loves a cheerful giver. "Every man according as he purposeth in his heart, *so let him give*; not grudgingly, or of necessity: for God loveth a cheerful giver" (2 Corinthians 9:7). It is pretty amazing that God doesn't just *like* a cheerful giver but *loves* one. Don't we all desire that special place with the Lord? We want to help our children learn to give and be generous as the Lord prompts and directs—both to the Lord for His work and to others.

Yes, tithing cuts down on savings, and yes, it isn't directly commanded in the New Testament, but Jesus was supportive of tithing. "Woe unto you, scribes and Pharisees, hypocrites! for ye pay tithe of mint and anise and cummin, and have omitted the weightier *matters* of the law, judgment, mercy, and faith: these ought ye to have done, and not to leave the other undone" (Matthew 23:23). Jesus told them that they should tithe and not neglect the weightier matters of the law.

We believe it is a good and blessed practice that we offer at least a tenth of our gross income to the Lord. We want to teach our children to tithe and even to give beyond the tithe, believing that giving is an important part of life in Christ and good financial stewardship.

"Honour the LORD with thy substance, and with the firstfruits of all thine increase: So shall thy barns be filled with plenty, and thy presses shall burst out with new wine" (Proverbs 3:9-

10). When our children learn to put the Lord first with their finances, the Lord says that He will bless in return.

In the process of teaching our children to be savers and not spenders, we do not want to turn them into cheap, hoarding misers with a money focus. They can save but still be generous when the Lord puts a need on their heart that they are to meet. "Let him that stole steal no more: but rather let him labour, working with *his* hands the thing which is good, that he may have to give to him that needeth" (Ephesians 4:28).

We regularly have missionaries stay with us. When they leave here our sons, who are (or were) saving for houses, have often sent them off with checks in their pockets or a vehicle that has been taken to the shop for some necessary maintenance. Two of our sons take the family out to eat when we are on vacation, and sometimes at home they will invite a sister or brother out to eat. They enjoy buying birthday and Christmas presents for family members. Joseph gifted the family with a Vitamix when we began pursuing better nutrition. The other day John was downtown near our local tea shop. That night at Bible time there was a little note and package beside his younger sister's seat. He had bought some of her favorite tea and told her how much he appreciated her. Those are just a few examples of how generosity can be paired with a savings mindset.

Tests of the Heart

In chapter 3, we discussed the foundation for a debt-free house is a young man whose heart is seeking first the kingdom of God and His righteousness. As he starts toward a goal of a debt-free house and begins to have money in his bank account, he may find himself becoming focused on his finances more than on the Lord. "He that trusteth in his riches shall fall: but the righteous shall flourish as a branch" (Proverbs 11:28). Help him be wary of that pitfall and avoid it by trusting fully in the Lord, serving Him first. A bank account big enough to buy a debt-free house isn't worth a heart that becomes money-driven and stingy, filled with worry and stress over his finances.

To avoid being caught up in the snares of the love of money when he begins working and saving, a young man must seek the Lord, spend time in His Word, and look for ways to serve Him. "For the love of money is the root of all evil: which while some coveted after, they have erred from the faith, and pierced themselves through with many sorrows" (1 Timothy 6:10).

Good Spending

In addition to giving there is other good spending. One of these is using earned income to purchase necessary work-related equipment with the goal of being more efficient and profitable. Our sons should weigh the cost and benefit before making any purchase.

When two of our sons started a remodeling business, they needed a pickup truck and some basic tools. They had to dip into their savings, but it was done with the plan that the equipment would generate income to pay itself back plus additional income. A young man who is using computers vocationally will have to spend money keeping his computer and software updated. If a young man is a self-employed auto mechanic, he needs tools for his job. This investment of money should recoup itself and allow the young man to continue to save.

How Will He Exercise the Power of Choice?

These years while our children are in our home provide us the wonderful opportunities to teach them the importance of saving their money. When they want to buy something, we can help them determine if it is a need or a want and give them the mindset of not purchasing just for a want. As children this might be only $10 or $20 that they have available to spend, but we are instilling habits of good stewardship with their finances.

The life we are encouraging is a life walking in the Spirit. "*This* I say then, Walk in the Spirit, and ye shall not fulfil the lust of the flesh" (Galatians 5:16). So many "needs" will vanish if we are walking in the Spirit. Steve's "need" of a new car for commuting was no need. He needed reliable transportation but not necessarily a new car. We lay needs before the Lord. He will either affirm it as a need and show us how He wants to provide for it or help us see that it really isn't a need at all.

There will be a constant tug-of-war between saving and spending. Perhaps we could use an analogy that walking in the Spirit equates with saving and walking in the flesh with spending. Of course that isn't always true, but it could hold when we are talking about using money for things that aren't needs.

The flesh loves to be catered to, thrilled, and lavishly dressed and dined.

We can play a significant role in whether our children are spenders or savers. If they are savers, they will need less income and have more money available to give to the Lord and to prepare their children (your grandchildren!) for life.

Financial conflicts in marriage are a significant predictor of divorce. Help your children avoid that pain and heartache.

When we open our home to our young adult children to live in while they are working and saving toward a house and marriage, we enable them to save much more quickly than if they were living on their own.

We don't believe you will find these things difficult as you raise your children. Living them out in your own lives provides an instant role model for your children, reinforcing what you are saying to them. It all starts when they are young, and it is worked out in their 20s. We encourage you to catch the vision now and begin heading down the road that allows your sons to do the impossible—own a house debt-free before marriage.

Chapter 6 Questions

- What is the maximum your son can save each month?
- What are ways you see your son limiting his spending?
- How can you help him to minimize it even more?
- What are examples of times you have seen your son with a willingness to wait on the Lord to provide for his needs and

times he has spent his money on something that wasn't a need?

- What are ways your family can learn to wait on the Lord for His provision for needs?

- What have you taught your son that he otherwise would have to pay others to do?

- What can you teach your son or learn with him that will save him having to hire the job out to professionals?

- Have you extended the offer of living at home for free to your son?

- Does your son tithe?

- Does he give to the Lord above his tithe?

- Is he generous?

- What are ways you can help your son not have a money focus as he saves for his house?

7 ARE SAVINGS ROBBERS AT WORK?

When Joshua was growing up, his parents always taught him to trust God for his needs. As Joshua had his personal time in the Word every morning and then twice a day together with the family, he saw Scripture affirm over and over that we are to trust God for His provision. During his Bible reading Joshua was convicted that borrowing is not trusting God's provision. Therefore, Joshua committed in his heart not to borrow, even for a house. His desire is to purchase his home debt-free to be a testimony of God's faithful provision to others and to bless his future family.

Joshua is 16 and acquiring skills in several business endeavors. Currently, he and his siblings are raising Nigerian dwarf goats. It all began with a need. For health reasons, his siblings were drinking rice milk, but they didn't care for the flavor. One of them had the idea to ask their parents if they could raise goats because goat milk tasted much better. They now have a small herd of eight goats, and they sell the new kids that are born. He realizes that he won't buy a house with their goat proceeds, but he is learning valuable business skills in the process such as salesmanship, managing resources, and bookkeeping.

Joshua also has a leather-working business. This gives him the opportunity to learn product design, quality assurance, sales, and customer service skills. He's able to make $15 an hour and is looking to increase this hourly income.

Joshua has taken ITonRamp's A+ course and successfully tested for his A+ credential. He is purchasing broken computers, fixing them, and reselling them to enhance his practical computer repair skills. He will soon be expanding his computer business services to those in his area, which will give his hourly income a real boost. He is planning to take ITonRamp's Network Plus and Security Plus courses to deepen his computer and network skills.

What Is the Main Savings Robber?

In this chapter, we identify what could be the main reason debt-free houses are not the norm but rather a rare occurrence for young men in our society. Most young men don't make the choices Joshua has been making from a young age. His parents taught him to trust the Lord, work hard, have a goal, be content, be frugal, and be patient. The outcome is a young man who utilizes his time serving the Lord, learning skills, working, and earning money. Joshua has the commitment, the plan, and the drive. It will be exciting to watch him approach his goal in the years ahead.

What are other boys his age doing? We wonder if most young men choose to use their time and their money pursuing fun and entertainment. Entertainment has almost become an idol in our culture today. Without Scriptural teaching and parental leadership, the teen years offer a vast array of pleasures, and young men often have finances available to pursue those activities. Entertainment and pleasure-seeking may be the greatest obstacle a young man must overcome en route to a debt-free house.

We couldn't possibly cover all the enticing entertainment-oriented savings and time robbers, but we will try to hit some of the major ones so that you will understand exactly the dangers we are talking about.

TV and Movies

Sitting in front of a TV and watching general programing or movies might be the least costly entertainment available. We have seen studies, however, indicating the average American watches almost seven hours a day! Ignoring the harm viewing TV and movies does to a person's soul, if we used the minimum wage of $7.25 per hour, that equals $50.75 every day in lost wages. In the course of a year, that represents a take-home pay of $14,628, which added to an income tax refund, would equal a yearly income of $16,168 (2013 tax, excludes other income).

What if that was invested in missions or saved for old age? Obviously few will work all day and then another seven hours in the evening, but if we apply any value to our time, we would conclude that TV is a huge waste.

One day Steve was waiting while a mechanic did some work on our car. A TV was playing in the corner of the waiting area, and he noticed a commercial. A family was shown "inhaling" luscious, sauce-dripping, cheese-flowing pizza. You could all but taste that delicious pizza. Steve found himself craving pizza just as the advertisers were hoping he would. If our children watch commercials, they will very likely want to spend their money on what is being advertised. Advertising works!

We want to teach our children to value their time and be productive with it. They need to see that how they spend their time is a tradeoff.

Hanging Out with Buddies

How our children spend their time in childhood and youth affects the rest of their lives. Hanging out with their friends might be enjoyable, but is it beneficial? "Foolishness *is* bound in the heart of a child …" (Proverbs 22:15). Youth have a way of wasting time and money when they are together, and their activities regularly lead to trouble.

"He that tilleth his land shall be satisfied with bread: but he that followeth vain *persons is* void of understanding" (Proverbs 12:11). This verse endorses our sons learning to work rather than "goofing around" with their friends. The word "vain" here simply means "empty" according to *Strong's Exhaustive Online Dictionary*. Have you noticed how silly and goofy teenage boys often are when they get together? This is not the way to train sons to be mature and godly. We want to raise children who are wise and make wise decisions rather than ones devoid of understanding.

Sports

Sports are as exciting as they are entertaining and addicting. If they weren't, people wouldn't spend such incredible amounts of time and money on them. Some use the famous British Olympic medal winner Eric Liddell as an example of why sports are good. But let's think about it.

What if Eric Liddell had spent all the hours he trained for the Olympics instead for the Lord? He lived only 45 years. On one occasion when he returned to Britain from his missionary work, he was asked if he ever regretted his decision to leave behind the fame and glory of athletics. Liddell replied, "It's natural for a chap to think over all that sometimes, but I'm glad I'm at the work I'm engaged in now. A fellow's life counts for far more at this than the other."

Don't confuse exercise with sports. It is beneficial to teach our sons to exercise briefly each morning and then move on to profitable use of their time. "For bodily exercise profiteth little: but godliness is profitable unto all things, having promise of the life that now is, and of that which is to come" (1 Timothy 4:8).

Giving our sons the appetite for sports is costly. It will consume valuable time and finances that could be given to serving the Lord or working toward a debt-free home. For more information on sports, we recommend our audio title *Sports—Friend or Foe*.

Cars and Trucks

We parents clearly understand how expensive it is to own a vehicle, which costs every month whether it is driven or not. The reality, though, is that once a car is owned, it begs to be driven and for many presents a temptation to invest in bells and whistles to spiff up the vehicle. As soon as you drive it, the costs start climbing due to fuel, maintenance, and the activities to which it is driven. The longer you can delay a car purchase, the less your son will spend and the more he will save.

We set a family policy that our sons needed to pay for their own car insurance when they wanted to get a driver's license. That necessitated a steady income. We found our sons were frugal and deferred driving until they had a need for their own transportation. That usually happened around 18.

When your son is ready for a car, encourage him to find a used, reliable, and inexpensive vehicle that he can work on himself. Help guide him to something practical with inexpensive parts.

We have heard families justify a son's car purchase because he had a job and needed a car. They went on to mention that the job was flipping burgers somewhere. Those types of jobs pay so little that the job hardly justifies a vehicle. By the time your son pays $100 a month on car insurance and another $100 on fuel, it would likely have been better for him to continue learning skills that would net a better paying job. When our sons began working, they typically earned more per hour than their electrical engineer father when he left corporate America. We would encourage you to inspire your sons to learn skills so that when they begin to work, they will earn a reasonable wage.

Big-Boy Toys

Motorcycles, jet skis, boats, airplanes, four-wheelers, ATVs, dirt bikes—what fun things there are to spend money on these days! Are those things sin? No, not unless the Lord has specifically directed a person not to spend money on them. Like so many other things, however, they are highly addictive and will consume our son's time and money. "Train up a child in the way he should go: and when he is old, he will not depart from it" (Proverbs 22:6). If young men develop appetites for those things growing up, they will not only consume time and finances now but also in the future. Think about that ongoing drain of time and money and the desire to spend time away from the family. Train them up now with godly desires, and they won't have to retrain themselves later.

Hunting and Fishing

There is nothing "wrong" with hunting and fishing. If a man neglects raising his children, though, in the nurture and admonition of the Lord because he is away from home hunting and fishing, that is sinful. Ephesians 6:4 is a clear command to fathers. "And, ye fathers, provoke not your children to wrath: but bring them up in the nurture and admonition of the Lord." As we have traveled this country giving conferences, we have seen time and again a man by himself out fishing. Is it possible he has a wife and children who would love to spend time with Dad? What does his equipment cost him? Are there better ways he could use that time and money?

We also hear from moms who are struggling with the constant responsibility of young children without support from their husbands. One example she might share will be that her husband leaves for several long weekends, or more, a year to go hunting.

If we give our sons the appetite for these pleasurable activities, we will give them the desire for something that is not only costly, time-consuming, and addictive but will perhaps keep them from being the fathers the Lord would have them be. There is only so much time in a day. How will your son spend his time?

Computers and Phones

Video games and their online counterparts are another entertaining use of time that we hear is highly addictive. We have spoken to numerous moms at conferences who share that their husbands come home from work only to spend all evening playing video games. We are also told that some games are evil and not only waste time but also poison the mind. "Finally, brethren, whatsoever things are true, whatsoever things *are* honest, whatsoever things *are* just, whatsoever things *are* pure, whatsoever things *are* lovely, whatsoever things *are* of good report; if *there be* any virtue, and if *there be* any praise, think on these things" (Philippians 4:8).

Internet surfing and social media can also hog huge amounts of time that we could otherwise use productively. Time once spent is gone forever. Will we raise sons who desire to spend their time productively now and with their children in the future as opposed to giving in to time and savings robbers?

Amusement Parks

Steve has loved amusement parks all his life. Yet, it has been over 20 years since we have gone to one. Are they evil? Most aren't. So what's the problem? Amusement parks never satisfy. They never say "enough." One thrill begs for another and another, bigger and more exciting each year.

There is a water park about 12 miles from our home. Driving by, we've noticed they are putting in a new attraction—a water slide that is at least six stories tall! We can only imagine how fast someone would be moving on that slide. What a thrill! Amusement parks are relatively costly even with a season pass, which must be used often to justify them. Then there are all the expensive treats one buys while there. Even if the cost wasn't high, it still takes time that could be used serving the Lord, earning income, or learning skills.

Designer Clothes

Since God clothed Adam and Eve in the Garden, clothing has been a necessity. There is a very broad spectrum of clothing available today from nice clothes to designer clothes. Men's shoes range in price from under $20 to the outrageously expensive $1,000, with a vast array of prices in between. One could pay over $100 for men's jeans while a normal pair of jeans might cost about $20. If our sons acquire a taste for expensive clothes, they are going to have far less money to save for a house. We can teach them to be content with clothing in a reasonable price range, to look for sales, to shop at thrift stores, and not to focus on pride in their outward appearance.

Food, Addictive Substances, and Sleep

Most of us acknowledge the expense and addictive qualities of smoking, alcohol, or drug abuse and direct our children away from such things. These substances waste not only money but time. Add in the long-term health repercussions that can gobble up huge amounts of money, rob a man of his ability to provide for his family, and consume precious time.

Those are obvious problems, but the not-so-obvious come in the form of normal food that we all must eat every day. If we don't help our children make healthy choices of food, they will be susceptible to many forms of disease such as obesity, diabetes, and heart disease. With almost any disease you research, you will find the way to overcome or avoid it is: eat healthy food, lose weight, stop smoking, stop drinking, and exercise.

"For the drunkard and the glutton shall come to poverty: and drowsiness shall clothe *a man* with rags" (Proverbs 23:21). In addition to alcohol, unhealthy food, and overeating, Scripture also warns about sleeping too much. Our children will avoid many health pitfalls if they heed those admonitions, and they will thus save the money and time that must be spent when health fails.

Dating

Dating is EXPENSIVE! Going for a walk on a date went out of fashion in the 1940s. Nowadays it seems that everything couples do on a date is expensive. If that wasn't enough, once your son starts dating, he is going to want to get married all the sooner. Give your children a vision to avoid dating and to embrace courtship. Courtship is responsibly building a relationship in a God-and-parent honoring way when the young people are prepared for marriage. Courtship eliminates dating and only establishes a relationship when your son is ready to be married after the Lord has directed him to the right one. One of the blessings of courtship is that it will typically be far cheaper than dating.

Are They Walking in the Spirit?

There is so much in our world today to draw time and money away from what is productive. The more time and money spent on entertainment and things that are unnecessary or unhealthy, the less that is available for serving the Lord, learning skills, earning income, and saving for a debt-free house.

As parents we have the opportunity to direct our children's hearts away from appetites that will consume their time and finances through life. "Even a child is known by his doings, whether his work *be* pure, and whether *it be* right" (Proverbs 20:11). We have the ability to launch our children toward not only financial success but also spiritual success.

What the flesh desires is costly, but walking in the Spirit is free and yields blessed fruit. This way of life is neither difficult nor expensive. It is something every one of us can do. Have we convinced you? It is worth it!

Chapter 7 Questions

- What entertainment does your son participate in?
- How much time does he spend on that entertainment?
- What sports is your son involved in?
- What other time and savings robbers might he have?
- What could he do more profitably with time that is currently given to time robbers?

8 WHAT SKILLS WILL HE HAVE?

Have you met Eric? You'd remember him if you had. He's a likable, enthusiastic, hard-working young man. He is the third child in a family with four boys and four girls. His heart's desire is to seek first the kingdom of God.

Eric's family is very musical, and he started playing the cello when he was six. In the early years, his family would sing and perform with their instruments at local retirement and nursing homes. By the time Eric was 10 years old, the four oldest children formed a string quartet and began performing professionally for weddings and also had prestigious, high-end background music jobs.

When Eric was 14, he saw an article in a gardening magazine about raising bees. He asked his parents if he could become a beekeeper. They approved the plan provided that he did the research and used his own money. First, Eric read everything he could on the subject of beekeeping. Then he found a local man who was retiring from beekeeping who sold him four hives and equipment at a very reasonable cost. Eric was now a beekeeper.

The first year the bees did well, and Eric harvested over 200 pounds of honey. By catering to those interested in health foods and locally produced products, he took advantage of a niche market and sold the honey at a premium.

Eric spent time finding creative ways to get the word out about his honey. In an effort to invest in others' lives and share about God's creation, Eric gave bee presentations in schools and libraries. He also made and marketed lip balm, furniture polish, and candles. Since the business was a small cottage industry, most of the complex government regulations didn't apply to him. Through the years, he was able to expand his honey operation to more than 30 beehives.

The bee business was a way for Eric to bring in a small income and be productive with his time while he was still busy in school. He estimates that over the years, he earned $8,000 to $10,000 from his beekeeping. His share of the quartet appearances yielded another $5,000.

New Ventures

At 16 most young men want a car, but Eric wanted a cow. That's right, a cow! Their family lived on the edge of the suburbs, but their yard was one acre. Again, after careful research and saving his money, Eric received his parents' permission to buy a young heifer. All was well for a while. Then the cow grew, and the reality of a cow living in the backyard where little children played proved too much. Eric's dad said the cow needed a new home.

Eric started knocking on doors in their neighborhood and soon found a neighbor who was willing to let the cow live on her open three-acre pasture. She also gave Eric permission to keep a companion cow, which he promptly purchased from a local dairy. Overnight, Eric was in the dairy business, milking five to six gallons of fresh whole milk a day. With a market of clients seeking healthy local products, a new business was born. Within a few years, the operation grew to three Jersey milk cows and a small herd of dairy goats with more than 100 hand-milked gallons of milk a week, supplying over 40 customers. Milking at five a.m. and five p.m. every day, in addition to his school and other work, kept Eric pretty busy.

Eric delighted in his interactions with his customers and sought any opportunity to encourage them because some were quite sick and needed the raw milk for their health. Also, he treasured the time with his younger brother who daily worked beside him in the milking operation. The other siblings would pitch in and help when it came to washing milk bottles or driving supplies to the neighbor's pasture. His family benefited from being able to drink any milk that wasn't sold.

Eric bought day-old Holstein bull calves from friends at the local dairy. He contacted Chick-fil-A about a petting zoo using the calves. If you have seen Chick-fil-A ads, you understand why they would want a Holstein petting zoo. When the calves were old enough to be weaned, Eric sold them.

Eric always looked for needs and constantly learned skills to meet those needs. Every day presented new opportunities. Over the course of five years, by the age of 21, his milk operation and the raising and selling of cattle allowed him to save close to an additional $10,000.

Into Real Estate

When Eric was 19 he studied, tested, and obtained his real estate license and began work under a local broker. It was a difficult time in real estate with a very soft market. He learned, however, to work hard in the midst of a bad economy, and when the market stiffened in later years his same work ethic yielded great dividends.

Eric sold about 18 homes in his first three years during very lean times in the housing market. Then with good market experience and a desire to save the costly brokerage fees, Eric began considering other brokerage options. At the age of 24 and with a desire to honor God in his business, he began his own real estate brokerage.

Years earlier as a young child, Eric had watched his parents work hard to get out of debt, and that made quite an impression on him. He decided he wanted to buy his house and live debt-free. As a realtor, Eric kept his eyes open for a house he might be able to buy with the cash he had been saving.

Because of a slow market during the fall months, a significantly undervalued town home was listed at $79,900. It was presented as a "short sale," and Eric wrote an offer on it in October. A "short sale" is when more is owed on the mortgage than the property is currently worth. Short sales take much longer to close because of many paperwork hoops and the potentially long amount of time it takes for lien-holder approval. It was mid-April before the two lien-holding banks approved his offer.

The house is a two-bedroom, one-bath, 900-square-foot town home in the Denver area. Eric is renting it out for $1,150 a month until he is married. Now that the housing market is beginning to recover, a similar town home in his neighborhood has been listed for $150,000. God gets the glory.

Where Did It Start?

Eric's dad read our book *Preparing Sons to Provide for a Single-Income Family* years ago and was quick to encourage his sons to gain practical skills and seek to meet the needs of others. Eric's grandpa taught him how to manage business books and develop business plans.

Eric sees young men around him acquire money and then spend it on gadgets and entertainment with seemingly no thought for the future. He feels it is important to live frugally, buy what is needed, and be generous in giving. He doesn't give with the motive to get back from God, but he has observed how God does give back.

Eric is a powerful example of a young man who is always learning and developing marketable skills. Eric made a statement that is dead on: "Things are for a season, and then you must be ready to move on." This mindset yields a vocationally well-rounded and marketable individual.

Will He Win the Lottery?

Lotteries have become popular as a get-rich-quick dream. No doubt a few win, but the odds of winning Powerball, for example, are roughly 1 in 175 million. Personally we wonder if the lottery and gambling have been fueled by years of daytime, win-it-big, game shows where contestants excitedly jump up and down and hoot and holler as they hope to strike it rich.

A get-rich-quick scheme is not God's way to make money. "Wealth *gotten* by vanity shall be diminished: but he that gathereth by labour shall increase" (Proverbs 13:11). God has ordained that a man work for his income. "For even when we were with you, this we commanded you, that if any would not work, neither should he eat" (2 Thessalonians 3:10).

To earn money a man must have skills. The more skilled he is in areas that are marketable, the better his income potential. The less skilled he is, however, the less he will normally make. If we desire that our sons make a livable wage and also have time to spend with their families, discipling their children, they need marketable skills.

Will the Last Person Leaving Seattle Turn Out the Lights?

So read a 1971 billboard sponsored by Bob McDonald and Jim Youngren after a severe economic downturn hit the city. Boeing had been flying high with a 1968 employment of over 100,000 employees. In 1970, Boeing entered a 17-month stretch of not receiving a single new airplane order and, by late 1971, employment was down to 32,500. The entire Seattle area economy was decimated as the unemployment tsunami descended, crushing one company after another in its path.

Even in booming industries, unforeseen events occur such as a fuel crisis, weather disaster, or terrorism. Then many who were once securely employed are out of work with mortgages that can't be paid. Those with a variety of skills who are quick to learn, however, move on to other work.

Will He Retire There?

Jack Welch, a past CEO of the $25 billion General Electric Corporation, which at one time employed 404,000 people, said, "Any organization that thinks it can guarantee job security is going down a dead end. Only satisfied customers can give people job security. Not companies."[1]

---

1. John A. Byrne, Jack: *Straight from the Gut* (Business Plus, 2003), Kindle Edition, Locations 2047-2048.

Job security is a thing of the past. Marketability is a thing of the present. When one job market dies or changes, one must be able to adapt or find other work. Companies today are looking for ways to stay in business, which often means cutting costs everywhere they can. One common approach is to send jobs overseas where labor is cheap. From what we have observed through the years and read, most companies seek to have every job filled by the lowest wage earner they can find. That will likely include jobs of interest to your son.

It seems people tend toward wanting to be knowledgeable in only one area. They set sights on getting a college degree, going to work in a job, and living happily ever after. Working at one company for life was understood in the past as sort of an assumed lifetime employment contract. Jack Welch comments on that idea. "Those 'contracts' were based on perceived lifetime employment and produced a paternal, feudal, fuzzy kind of loyalty. If you put in your time and worked hard, the perception was that the company took care of you for life. As the game changed, people had to be focused on the competitive world, where no business was a safe haven for employment unless it was winning in the marketplace."[2]

Preparing Our Sons

We desire to help prepare our sons for life, and their vocational skills are an important part of that. Even with preteens, you can begin instilling these thoughts in your children's minds. Key to

---

2. John A. Byrne, Jack: *Straight from the Gut*, Kindle Edition, Locations, 2049-2052.

this is motivating your sons to be constantly learning, improving, and being marketable with an arsenal of skills they can use to generate income for their families.

Whether it be for employment or self-employment, skills are critical. Employers value those who are not only hardworking but also learning and growing. Since Eric was self-employed, he was able to move smoothly from one endeavor to another, gaining speed and capital as he went. His goal was to seek first the kingdom of God. He studied and learned new skills and began new endeavors. That is what is needed today.

The Apostle Paul was a tent maker. "Yea, ye yourselves know, that these hands have ministered unto my necessities, and to them that were with me" (Acts 20:34). He used his skills to support not only himself but others who traveled with him. He had a portable, marketable skill as he served the Lord Jesus. Work wasn't the focus of his life; it barely earned a sentence or two in Scripture. God used that income, though, to enable Paul to serve. Your son needs marketable skills that allow him to serve the Lord, save for a house before he is married, and then provide for his family.

Where to Begin?

You begin right where your son is, whatever your circumstances. Don't wait. Start now. The older your son, the more urgent the need to maximize the time that is left. If you haven't read *Preparing Sons to Provide for a Single-Income Family*, we suggest that you read it first because we won't repeat that information here. Then have your son read it.

One thing you can do is look for needs that require a skill to meet them. Here are some of our personal examples. In 1990 when we accepted leadership in our local homeschool group, Nathan, who was 13 at the time, agreed to provide the technical expertise to format and produce a newsletter while we provided the content. The study and acquisition of skills to accomplish that commitment is what began his career as an independent consultant in Information Technology.

When Christopher, 11, and Nathan, 13, began their lawn mowing business, Christopher agreed to do the business accounting. He studied and grew in accounting skills through the years, and that created opportunities for consulting with businesses that wanted to convert their handwritten accounting systems to software. He is now the chief financial officer of our family's business, Communication Concepts, and teaches ITonRamp Quickbooks classes in addition to his other duties.

Joseph was 10 when he began programming. Although there wasn't really a need at that point, Steve felt it would be a good skill for him to learn. After he developed some programming skills, Steve found programming projects that would challenge his growth.

Remember how Joshua (in the previous chapter) and his siblings began a herd of goats because they had a need for fresh raw milk. They learned much in the process such as animal husbandry, food product sanitation, marketing, bookkeeping, and customer service skills. Joshua even built some specialized goat-milking equipment and is now marketing that equipment to others with milking herds.

What Skills Do Dad and Mom Have?

Dads usually have some skills that are marketable and hence are able to earn an income for the family. Have you considered teaching your skills to your son? We know that an increasing number of moms have vocational skills when they come home from the workforce. Are there skills that Mom can teach your son?

Our children will learn the skills we teach them more quickly than other skills because we can direct their learning. When they have questions, they can go to Dad or Mom for the answers. Dad and Mom's experience factor goes beyond what a child can learn from books.

Steve's earlier career was as an electrical engineer with a systems emphasis. When the family converted an old bus into an RV, many systems-related issues had to be solved, and so we worked on them together. We installed a 15 KW generator, battery banks, dual inverters, and power distribution. With that interest piqued, Joseph and John went on to study the electrical code and sat for the electrical contractor's exam.

We rebuilt all the brakes and suspension and fixed a myriad of other mechanical problems to make the bus roadworthy. We installed new windows, repaired several windshields, and added air conditioning. We planned and installed fresh, gray, and black water systems. We designed and built the interior, including a sitting area, kitchen, bunk area, bathroom with shower, and a master bedroom. Joseph custom designed, built, and installed the cabinets. We removed a huge rusted-out X-frame tag axle suspension assembly. Steve calls the bus conversion a family shop class on wheels, and it has been a great tool in teaching the children a host of skills.

Map out a plan for learning new skills and make it a part of the daily homeschool schedule. With just one or two hours a day of their school time your children will make rapid progress in gaining skills.

It isn't necessary to do a scope and sequence for what you want to teach your son. Research online for textbooks that you can use. Go through the table of contents and highlight the areas that you deem essential for them to learn. Then look for projects that you can use to reinforce what they have learned. We believe you will get excited about what your son is learning at home under your direction.

Are There Other Projects?

We ran out of room for the necessary book storage for our Titus 2 ministry in the basement of our home and needed a larger basement. God led us to build our current house. After it was roughed in, the family went to work. We pulled over a mile of Romex and made connections, wired for the security system, installed all the plumbing and fixtures, hung the sheet rock, finished it, hung all the doors and trim, laid tile on the main floor, painted inside and out, put in a complete drainage system, poured and finished over 125 cubic yards of concrete external to the house and garage, and landscaped. All this work exposure has yielded young men who are competent to tackle a task. "I can do all things through Christ which strengtheneth me" (Philippians 4:13).

Actually, the young ladies have worked alongside the guys on these projects except for the bus mechanical work. All the children have a "can do" attitude in approaching any project that needs to be done. If we don't know how to do something, it just means it will take a little longer while we research what needs to be done.

What Skills Will He Have?

Wouldn't you love to have a son like Eric? That young man is going somewhere. He is not afraid of a venture and is determined to learn and grow. Don't we want to inspire that in our sons as well? Eric's parents didn't teach him those skills. They just motivated him.

While this book is targeted at young men, our daughters will certainly benefit from learning marketable skills. They can utilize them while still at home and in a husband's business should they marry.

Face it, times are changing and economic prospects are tough. Companies have had to do everything they can to lower costs and find inexpensive help. The key for our sons' future ability to earn income is that they are marketable with many skills.

Our roles as parents are critical in our children's lives. It isn't enough to ask them what they want to be when they grow up. We can use these vital years to equip them with marketable skills that will not only enable them to earn money to save for a debt-free house but also to provide for a family when they are married.

Chapter 8 Questions

- What skills does your son have?
- What skills are being developed?
- Have you read *Preparing Sons to Provide for a Single-Income Family*?
- What skills do you have that you can teach your son?
- What projects could you and your son work on to develop skills?

9 HOW TO ACQUIRE NECESSARY SKILLS

Jesse is our youngest son. At 19 years old, he hasn't saved enough to purchase a house debt-free yet, but he is making good, steady progress toward his goal. Jesse is a perfect example of a young man who is purposefully gaining marketable skills.

When Jesse was in high school, he took over the lawn maintenance for our family's yard. He studied fertilizers plus weed and pest control and learned what to do and when to apply specific agents. He also spearheaded the selection of trees best suited for our region and planted them in our yard according to his research. For several years he had a lawn service that several neighbors used, which started him on his earning and saving path. He also studied a small engine repair course so that he could maintain his equipment rather than pay others to do it.

As his older brothers needed assistance with their businesses, Jesse spent time studying and learning new skills so he was qualified to work for them. He learned HTML to work for his brother, Joseph, on websites. Next he studied AutoCad, a powerful computer-aided design program that John, another brother, uses in his business. Jesse now has a number of marketable skills and is earning between $30 and $45 an hour depending on which skill set he is using.

Will He Be Autodidactic?

Frankly, may we all be lifelong autodidacts. Autodidacts are people who are self-taught, self-learners. They aren't dependent on others to teach them because they are willing to study and learn for themselves. They research the best book or resource on a particular subject, and study it. This is the mindset we want our children to have toward acquiring skills. Being autodidactic saves both time and money.

Here is a partial list of skills and credentials that one or more members of our family have taught themselves:

Computer Programming

HTML/CSS
Javascript
C#
PHP

HOW TO ACQUIRE NECESSARY SKILLS

    Objective C
    SQL

Other skills

    Photography
    Drawing
    Graphic design
    Typography
    Layout and design
    Writing children's books
    Creating eBooks
    Computer aided design - AutoCad

Information Technology

    Microsoft Certified IT Professional Server Administrator
    Microsoft Certified Technology Specialist
    Microsoft Certified Systems Administrator
    Microsoft Certified Systems Administrator: Messaging
    Microsoft Certified Systems Engineer
    Microsoft Certified Professional
    CompTIA A+
    CompTIA Network+
    CompTIA Security+
    Certified Novell Administrator
    Certified Novell Engineer
    QuickBooks Certified User
    QuickBooks Certified ProAdvisor

Construction

> Trim carpentry
> Tiling
> Master electrician
> Master plumber
> Concrete finishing
> Residential chemical handling

Musical instruments

> Banjo
> Fiddle
> Guitar
> Mandolin
> Bass
> Piano

Information is constantly changing and to stay marketable one has to keep learning. There is no time to stop. Learning can be pleasurable and exciting. When one of our daughters was 19, she said, "There is so much to learn and so little time!" That was quite the wisdom from the lips of youth.

We would encourage you to create a home atmosphere where your children thrive on learning. Our first efforts go toward learning more about the Lord Jesus, and then we learn vocationally-related subjects. There are many ways to gain knowledge for skills in addition to learning from Dad or Mom. Let's explore some of these possibilities.

Books

Books are the foundational learning vehicle. We frequently make use of books for our autodidactic learning. When Joseph began learning computer programming, we bought an instructional book for him. John studied concrete work in high school from a book, and Jesse learned small engine repair. There is a book on almost any subject one would wish to study.

Most books can be ordered and delivered to your home in a few days. When researching a potential book purchase, we read the good and bad reviews. We want to hear why readers liked or disliked the book. In some cases the very reasons someone liked a book are reasons we wouldn't. If the reviewer loved the satire and earthy language, then we know we wouldn't care for it. The same is true for the negative reviews. The reasons the reviewer hated the book may be the very reasons we would enjoy it. If they gave a book a one star review because it used Scripture, then that tells us we would be pleased with the fact that the author used the Bible to support what he was saying.

Steve recently purchased a book by a well-known person. The reviews looked good and so did the introduction. When Steve had a chance to read the first few pages, however, he stopped because the author used crude language. Steve hopes the book review he submitted was helpful to others so that those who cared could avoid the vulgar language. Books are a great source for learning; however, do be careful what you are reading.

The library is also an option, but highlighting in a borrowed copy is frowned on! We regularly buy books because we consider them an investment in our futures.

Homeschool

We believe wholeheartedly that homeschool is the best form of education. We think textbooks lead our children toward an autodidactic life. That is one reason why we prefer textbooks for homeschooling. Our children learn to study on their own in school, and that prepares them for a lifetime of self-learning.

With homeschooling, we can tailor our children's education based on how God is leading. Especially in the high school years, two to three hours of our children's education time each day was spent in learning marketable skills. Right now our 17-year-old daughter is studying art through an online course. She was hired to illustrate a mini-book her older sister wrote and later this year will illustrate a full children's book.

The teen years are vitally important to young people for gaining skills. When they are homeschooled, they have many more hours available to devote to that learning.

Private School

Over 30 years ago, when our oldest children were young, two of them attended private Christian school for a short period. We found that the classroom setting and peer influences were undesirable, not to mention very costly. Through the years, we have had many parents share their experiences with private Christian schools and that information has affirmed our feelings.

In a private school, students spend their days learning what every other student is learning. They will receive little if any customized education and are seldom given several school hours each day to learn marketable skills.

Vocational School

From what we have heard and observed, the quality and environment of these schools vary greatly. Normally, the instructors have vocational experience but are typically not as credentialed as those teaching in colleges or maybe even public schools. That isn't necessarily a bad thing, but it is something that you might want to check into if that is important to you.

Often children who can't make it into college are channeled to vo-tech schools. If you are leaning in that direction for your children, we strongly encourage you to go and observe classes, including break times.

We knew a young man who appeared very solid in the Lord. His family enrolled him in vo-tech. Within six months, the young man was in deep spiritual trouble. We don't know whether they have succeeded in winning him back to the Lord. We would encourage any parent considering a vo-tech school to do his "homework" and be extremely cautious.

Online Courses

The world is at our children's fingertips, and they can research almost anything via their keyboards. A host of online courses are available—everything from decidedly Christian environments to secular college classes. Although most of these don't have peer-to-peer interactions, we are told that some do.

No matter what your budget, online classes are available. Many main-line colleges offer free courses but no credit is earned for them. For Christians who care, a significant challenge is avoiding the humanistic content in courses such as liberal arts and humanities classes. If they are from a secular college, they will likely have a humanistic foundation and some will be blatantly antagonistic toward Christian beliefs. Even if it is a benign subject such as math, the instructor's theological worldview will enter in through casual comments and examples. "For we wrestle not against flesh and blood, but against principalities, against powers, against the rulers of the darkness of this world, against spiritual wickedness in high *places*" (Ephesians 6:12).

What do you know about the organization and those doing the instructing? If they have a statement of faith, has each professor signed it? Do they teach evolution or creation? Just like the bumper sticker says, "The mind is a precious thing. Don't waste it." We plead with you to be on guard. Satan wants your children.

Apprenticeship

The very best and God-ordained apprenticeship is for Dad to apprentice his sons. "My son, hear the instruction of thy father, and forsake not the law of thy mother: For they *shall be* an ornament of grace unto thy head, and chains about thy neck" (Proverbs 1:8-9). When sons apprentice under their fathers, it is a win-win situation. The sons are gaining insight and instruction from their father, and Dad is being blessed by spending more time with his sons and deepening their relationship as he trains him.

What about your son apprenticing with a nice man you know? Certainly, that is far better than having him apprenticing with someone you don't know. Under no circumstances would we ever consider apprenticing a son with an unbeliever. Apprenticeship is in a way being yoked together. It is an even stronger relationship than the teacher-student one. "Be ye not unequally yoked together with unbelievers: for what fellowship hath righteousness with unrighteousness? and what communion hath light with darkness?" (2 Corinthians 6:14).

What about your son apprenticing for a godly Christian man you know? We have been told about two situations in which a son was apprenticed to a "godly Christian man from church" because the dad felt he didn't have sufficient skills to apprentice his son. In time, both families lost their sons to the worldly influence of the apprenticing man. The families weren't aware that the apprenticing man didn't agree with some of the family's convictions. As the other man and apprenticing son were working together and talking, the apprenticing man would share comments about the boy's parents' convictions and biblical teaching. He sowed seeds of doubt in the young man's mind about his parents. In time, the man invited the son to come and stay with his family, which is what ended up happening in both situations to the heartbreak of the parents.

Though we suspect these situations are the exception, we want parents to be aware of the risk. Prayerfully consider all such "opportunities," especially if it involves your son moving away. Even if he will be working for a great Christian organization, other young people will be there as well. Many parents send their troubled youth to such places hoping it will "fix" them. Your son may be in close proximity to a rebel for weeks. Is that something with which you are comfortable?

What if Dad doesn't think he has skills to apprentice his son? If that is the case, why not learn together? Then the two of you not only learn but also grow closer. With the deep desire of your heart for your son, he will gain skills. Reread the list of skills our children have. We did not need to go to others. We are autodidactic. "And, ye fathers, provoke not your children to wrath: but bring them up in the nurture and admonition of the Lord" (Ephesians 6:4). Dads and Moms, you can do it!

Is He Gifted Mentally?

A family told us that because their son was very bright they felt it best to send him to college. That certainly is their prerogative;

however, a bright young man also means one who will learn quickly under his parents' guidance. He can assimilate more difficult tasks and concepts with less of their involvement. That family hadn't taken advantage of the junior and senior high years in their son's life to help him gain valuable skills. Six years of prime time was gone as they simply looked ahead toward college. Had that son been learning skills, by the time he reached 18 he might have been a young entrepreneur with a successful, fledgling business and well on his way to saving for a house debt-free. His business might have continued to provide for him and for a family without the time and money spent on college.

Is He Gifted Physically?

Our two older sons were in sports until they were 11 and 13 years old. They were skilled ball players with much potential. We discovered, though, when we took them out of sports how much more productive they became with their time. We often laugh now and say, "Our boys didn't buy their houses debt-free because they could hit a ball."

The teen years are vital for learning skills and beginning to earn income. Most youth fritter those years away playing sports rather than choosing to invest their time in what will be productive for their future.

We've heard some say that their son is gifted physically and thus wants to play sports professionally. Even if your child is outstanding in his sport and avoids injury, the chances that he will become a professional athlete are very small according to an article that cited NCAA statistics.[1] For those who played high school basketball there is only a .03% chance of them making it to the pros. That means of the 156,000 male high-school seniors playing basketball, only 44 of them will be drafted. For football, the odds improve to .08%. Certainly, these are better odds than buying a Powerball ticket, but still it is very unlikely. It would seem wiser to use the critical teen years for gaining skills and earning money than pursuing sports.

Remember Eric Liddell's reflection on his years of sports? One pro ball player came up to Steve after a conference at which Steve made negative comments about sports. He said, "I agree. It's a pit. If I had another option at this time, I'd take it."

Make Informed Decisions

We want to raise children who are lifelong autodidacts. When your son is blessed to have a good job, whether employed or self-employed, he will still need to be learning and growing. We have a family friend who uses those exact words when asked how he is doing. May that be true for all of us.

There are many ways to learn, but they all start with a desire for gaining skills. Some of the ways we can learn are undesirable because of the negative influences that can come along with the education. Please don't assume that just because others are using a particular approach, it must be good. Each couple needs to seek the Lord and His Word for the best way to direct

---

1. Lynn O'Shaughnessy. "The Odds of Playing College Sports." http://www.cbsnews.com/news/the-odds-of-playing-college-sports/. April 2011.

their children toward gaining skills. May we all be informed consumers, carefully evaluating each avenue.

We are encouraging you to motivate your sons to the attainable goal of owning his first house debt-free. Could we also inspire you to do something else that many would say is also impossible—be the ones to teach your children skills or learn them together? Apprenticing your own children in the skills you have offers so many positives and avoids so many negatives that can come from sending them into another's influences. If you don't have the skills, find resources that you can learn together with your sons.

We didn't discuss college in this chapter. We felt that topic was too lengthy to add to this chapter, so we will discuss it next.

Chapter 9 Questions

- How has your son demonstrated that he is an autodidact?
- During the last year how many books has he read that will improve his marketable skills?
- How is your son developing further skills?

10 IS COLLEGE THE ANSWER?

When Brad was 13, his dad had a man-to-man talk with him. He asked Brad if he thought he would want to get married some day, and Brad said he thought he would. His dad shared how men need to be able to provide for their families, so the two of them wrote out a plan that would enable Brad to be able to support a wife by age 23. They projected that a reasonable wage to support a family would be $50,000 a year.

At 14, Brad's dad began taking him to his insurance agency. He taught him customer service and telephone skills after school each day. When he was 16, Brad graduated from their homeschool and began apprenticing under their pastor. He also started studying law with an online college.

When Brad was 18, he learned about an opportunity to sell credit card processing to small businesses. It was a long, slow, uphill climb before he finally began earning a little income. After seven months, his fourth paycheck was the first one to break $100. Over time his earnings per month grew. Eventually he was making $1,000, then $2,000, then $3,000–$4,000, and finally $5,000 a month. By his third year, at 21 years old, he was close to his $50,000 a year target.

At this point, Brad also became interested in gold and silver coins and started a business selling them. He aggressively pursued this new endeavor via word-of-mouth, gun shows, and even Craigslist. In the next two years, his income from this venture surpassed his credit-card servicing income. Now at 26, with his coin business continuing to grow, he has hired his sisters and dad to help.

Brad has just been married and would have no problem writing a check for his house although he has decided to rent for a time. He has been a careful saver and a hard worker. There is such peace when one has been a responsible steward and is able to enjoy the fruits thereof. As busy as the business has kept him, he still spends a significant amount of time helping his pastor. Brad has managed his priorities well in seeking first the kingdom.

We didn't finish the story about Brad's online law classes. He only took a few, but during that time he saw the potential income from the credit card processing and came to a realization. It would be better for him to invest time in his business during these years and then, once established, he could easily get a degree if he wanted one. So he stopped taking the college classes.

Now, he is able to look back and see how wise that decision was. With his two businesses, he has no need for a degree. It would simply have consumed time and money that was much better utilized elsewhere.

A Hindrance

This may be surprising and perhaps even shocking, but a college education can be a great hindrance to purchasing a debt-free house. The amount of time and money one invests in college makes it extremely difficult for a young man to purchase a home debt-free before he is 30.

Our boys built their businesses during what would usually be college years. They earned and saved money while not spending it on a college education. By the time they would have graduated from college, they had saved enough, or almost enough, to purchase a house debt-free, and they were ahead of their peers in establishing their businesses. It seemed like the best of both worlds—a business of their own and avoidance of the negative influences and cost of a college degree.

We had both gone to college and were very aware of the worldly influences there. We didn't want those influences in our children's lives. While Teri didn't use her degree, choosing instead to stay home and raise our children, Steve spent 20 years in the corporate world. When he was able to start his own business, he was much happier than when he was employed by corporations. No longer was he asked to compromise biblical principles and thereby experience conflict with his employer because he couldn't do what they wanted him to do. He was able to run his business as the Lord would have him and eliminated hours and hours each day of bombardment from the world. We desired those same positive, self-employment, spiritual advantages for our sons.

Our sons have gladly not gone to college. We shared with them reasons not to want to go to college based on our personal experiences there. They have observed many others who have gone to college and seen negative fruit in their lives. Our sons have been pleased with not attending college. They have homes debt-free and avoided the negative influences and high costs of college.

A Financial Perspective

A college education is costly. It will most likely delay or eliminate a young man's efforts to save money for a house at least for the college season. The national average for in-state tuition at a four-year college in 2013-2014 was $8,893, and for the full four years, it was $35,572. With room and board, the cost rose to $73,564[1].

---

1. Trends in Higher Education, trends.collegeboard.org.

IS COLLEGE THE ANSWER?

Perhaps you plan to pay for your son's college education, and you have saved the average of $75,000 it will take for him to get his degree. Let's assume that buying a house debt-free is one of your son's goals. He's 18 years old and has already managed to save $20,000. Now what if you made him the offer of a check for $75,000 (in reality doing so might incur gift taxes), income tax paid, in exchange for the commitment not to go to college. Would he take it? If he did, he would have $95,000 toward a house at only 18.

Perhaps your son heads down the college path with you financing his schooling. He is in his second year, and you find out that he isn't on track to graduate in four years. He is now one of the national average two-thirds of men who don't graduate in four years. It will take him two additional years to get his degree.

According to the National Center for Education Statistics, only 34.1% of the males entering a four-year college graduated in four years. The four-year diploma graduation rate for males in six years improves to 58.8%[2]! Do you think the parents of those young men budgeted for an extra two years of college costs? What about the fact that even after six years, 41% won't even graduate and have a diploma? The money has been spent, six years of income-producing time vanished, and no diploma is in hand. This is the reality of college graduation today.

---

2. http://nces.ed.gov/programs/digest/d12/tables/dt12_376.asp

Don't Forget Lost Income

When evaluating the expense of a four-year degree, you have to factor in college tuition, room and board, and other fees, but another major cost is often neglected. While your son is in school, he is not able to earn income. He will have four to six years of lost revenue. That can be a significant amount of money.

Total Lost Earnings*		
	Four years	Six years
$15/hr	$ 96,988	$145,482
$20/hr	$124,126	$186,195
$25/hr	$150,109	$225,164
$40/hr	$227,548	$341,322
$50/hr	$278,331	$417,497

*Assumes 40 hour weeks, 1 exemption, KS income tax, 52 weeks/year

Now think about this scenario. If your son was living at home with minimal expenses during those years and working instead of going to college how easily could he save all that he needs to purchase his home debt-free.

Will He Incur School Debt?

What if your son has to finance his own college education, runs out of money, and his only option to complete school is taking on student debt? The average member of the college graduating class of 2011 in the U.S. borrowed $26,600 during college according to American Student Assistance. Using an online loan payment calculator, if his loan rate was 3.4% for a term of 10 years, his monthly payment would be $262. The total amount of interest he would pay is $4,816! That payment of $262 added to your son's normal monthly spending will have a significant impact on his ability to save toward a debt-free house. To consider the true impact of borrowed money, remember it takes tax-paid funds to pay down debt.

Most assume, though, that they will earn a much higher income with a college diploma and will thus be able to repay their loan easily. Therefore they are more willing to take on student debt. With the right degree, of course, that is sometimes the case, but there is no guarantee.

One dad with an engineering undergraduate degree and a master's in business administration can't find work. He has over $140,000 in school loans waiting to be repaid. He said it was easy to obtain the loans, and he was assured that with his credentials repayment would not be a problem. The loan officer's assurances provide him with little comfort as he continues to look for work.

Dr. Sue, in her late 40s, is our podiatrist. In speaking with her, we learned that she would love to be home with her two children, but cannot because she has $325,000 in debt from medical school loans that must be paid—and this amount is down from the $425,000 that she first owed! Her husband is also a podiatrist with a similar amount of school debt.

Dr. Sue now works as little as possible so that she can meet her school loan obligation each month. Her heart is at home, and yet she is in bondage to her loans.

Job Assurance?

Will his degree get him a job? Maybe, maybe not. Google "are college grads getting jobs." Steve has been researching this topic extensively. Parents considering sending their sons to college need to know what the secular world is saying about jobs after college. Innumerable articles discuss the increased difficulty graduates are having finding jobs in their degree fields. Degrees in business, English, history, and perhaps even marketing will likely yield disappointing results when job hunting.

Here are a few recent personal examples. In Chicago, a young man picked us up with our rental car. We found out he had a B.S. in marketing. After graduation, he couldn't find an opening in his field so he took a job making $10 an hour with the rental car agency until he could find a better position.

Not long after that, a very pleasant young man was waiting on us at a local restaurant. We began talking with him and found out he had a four-year business degree. He had spent a long time job hunting after graduation without success. When his money ran out, he started waiting on tables for $15 an hour including tips. He told us that unless you know someone who could get you into a company or had higher level degrees, job prospects in his field were not good.

Another example is a homeschooled young man who had his heart set on being an architect. His family didn't have the money to pay for his college, so he borrowed. He assumed he wouldn't have a problem repaying the loan since architects earn a good income. He graduated and found a job paying a reasonable wage.

Because the housing crunch hit, however, he was laid off after a year and a half of work. When he could not find any other architect jobs, he joined the police force. He is now trying to pay down his $100,000 school debt on a law-enforcement salary.

College degrees are not the guaranteed source of income they were a decade or two ago. The market is becoming saturated with individuals with four-year degrees. Brad Voeller, CEO of College Plus, says that the B.S. has become a commodity[3].

In *College Unbound*[4], Jeffrey Selingo reports that the number of people receiving master's degrees in 2009 was double what it was in the 1980s. He states that the bachelor's degree has become the new high-school diploma, and it's only a matter of time before the doctorate is the new master's degree. It's called "credential" creep, and it's rampant today in almost every career field.

Should your son find that a B.S. is insufficient to get the job he really wants, have you saved enough to be able to send him for his master's or PhD? Check out the high-priced tuitions for master's and PhD studies. We would encourage you to

---

3. Interview with Andrea Swartz, December, 23, 2010, http://www.notablepeople.org/blog/2010/12/interview-with-brad-voeller-of-college-plus/.

4. Jeffrey J. Selingo. *College Unbound: The Future of Higher Education and What It Means for Students* (New Harvest, 2013), Kindle Edition, Page 10.

do some online searches on underemployment. Also do your own personal surveys. When you are out, ask people whether they went to college, what their major was, and what their job experience has been. Informed consumers make better decisions.

Will He Earn a Large Salary?

Most people go to college to assure themselves of a job with high wages. We recently heard about a young man who earned a four-year business degree but hasn't been able to find a job in his field. Instead of taking a lower paying position, though, he sits home all day.

Having a college degree is often viewed as a ticket to making "big bucks." According to Wikipedia's list of college-dropout billionaires, their average worth is three times that of billionaires with PhDs. The article also reported that 20% of American's millionaires never attended college.

The National Association of Colleges and Employers[5] states that the average salary for 2013 graduates was $45,327. For education it was $40,337 and for humanities and social services it was $37,791 ($18/hr). That may not sound too bad, but consider this from a *CNN Money* article by Tami Luhby on June 25, 2013: "Recent college grads face 36% 'mal-employment' rate."[6] The article states that more than one third of the recent college graduates took jobs that didn't require a degree. Consider the

---

5. http://www.naceweb.org/s09042013/salary-survey-average-starting-class-2013.aspx
6. Tami Luhby. "Recent College Grads Face 36% 'Mal-Employment Rate," http://money.cnn.com/2013/06/25/news/economy/malemployment-rate/index.html, June, 25, 2011.

statistics we cited above that almost half who start college never graduate. Of those who do graduate, one third end up taking a job that doesn't require a degree!

In reality, we don't want to raise our children with money as a focus, because 1 Timothy 6:10 says, "For the love of money is the root of all evil: which while some coveted after, they have erred from the faith, and pierced themselves through with many sorrows." They do need, however, to earn a livable wage that can support a family. We want you to catch a vision for how it is possible for your son to be successful in life without a college degree. This is a new thought for some.

Income Studies

We've read numerous articles promoting the financial benefits of a college degree. Often these researchers will compare an average income of those with a four-year college degree to those who only have a high school diploma.

We would encourage you to do your own Internet searches. You have to critically evaluate what you read from the various sources. Use search terms such as "compare four year grads to high school grads income" or "college grads earn more." When we did this, two articles, one above the other in the search results, stated opposite findings. To no surprise, we noticed that the college-generated articles are quite glowing about how much more grads make than non-grads. The educationally funded sites were also optimistic of grads' earning potential. These articles typically ignore some major financial statistics such as the person's lost income while in school, the percentage who have to go to school for six years, not four, in order to graduate, the significant number who never graduate, and the percentage of graduates taking jobs that don't require a degree.

One of the best articles on the subject we've read is from the *Wall Street Journal*, "College Does Pay Off, but It's No Free Ride."[7] Carl Bialik points out that those attending college are generally of a different caliber than those who don't. This criteria provides a sorting of the types of workers. Comparing apples to apples, *he indicates that the type of person who goes to college and graduates would also most likely be successful if he didn't go to college.*

For those of you who are homeschoolers, we'd like to share an example from a conversation we had with a restaurant owner. During the conversation he mentioned that he recruits homeschoolers to work in his restaurants. He felt they were far more motivated, responsible, and hardworking than others. In essence, the average homeschooler was not the average high school student. For those who may need data to affirm that your homeschooled children are above average, go to the National Home Education Research Institute's website, nheri.org.

Will He Learn to Think Critically?

Some will want their son to attend college so that he will learn to think critically. In *Academically Adrift: Limited Learning on College Campuses*, however, Arum and Roksa report sadly that

---

7. Carl Bialik. "College Does Pay Off, But It's No Free Ride." *Wall Street Journal*, http://online.wsj.com/news/articles/SB10001424052970203611404577046071107794292. November 19, 2011.

IS COLLEGE THE ANSWER?

"many students are not only failing to complete educational credentials; they are also not learning much, even when they persist through higher education. In general, as we have shown, undergraduates are barely improving their CLA-measured skills in critical thinking, complex reasoning, and writing during their first two years of college."[8]

It used to be that a degree was an indication of a level of educational achievement, even some degree of character, but that is no longer necessarily true given the current academic slide and grade inflation in most colleges. Steve recently spoke to a dad in a management position in a ten billion dollar manufacturing company. Steve asked him what he thought of the current college new-hires. The man said, "They are fantastic!" Steve was a bit surprised and told him that he had heard differently. "Oh, yes," the man responded, "the U.S. graduates haven't been very good lately, so we have begun hiring from overseas and bringing them here. The foreign new-hires are excellent for us."

What Will It Profit?

Another consideration when evaluating the decision for college would be the undermining of your son's faith. That faith is crucial for every aspect of his future including his business or employment and decisions regarding them. All that you have invested to help your son toward an obedient walk with Jesus Christ could be wiped out during his college years.

---

8. Richard Arum and Josipa Roksa. *Academically Adrift: Limited Learning on College Campuses* (University of Chicago Press, 2010). Kindle Edition, Locations 1169-1172.

Many will say, "My son is different. He can handle college. He won't lose his faith." Maybe, but he will be encountering the most powerful worldly force he has ever faced in his life.

According to what parents tell us and what Arum and Roksa affirm in *Academically Adrift*, "The student's peer group is the single most potent source of influence on growth and development during the undergraduate years."[9] They also indicated that next to the peer group, faculty are the most powerful factor in affecting your son. The pressure will be phenomenal for your son to change his worldview and faith. "For what is a man profited, if he shall gain the whole world, and lose his own soul? or what shall a man give in exchange for his soul" (Matthew 16:26)?

If he graduates, will it be worth it if he rejects Christ? "Be not deceived: evil communications corrupt good manners" (1 Corinthians 15:33). It is pretty amazing when even the secular studies agree with Scripture regarding the incredible power of peers. Academia insists it is for good. Scripture says it is for evil.

We have had countless parents tell us that one or more of their children lost their faith in college. The heartache in these families is unbelievable. For one daughter, it only took six months, and she was living at home while attending community college. The pressure is intense.

We just heard from a very distraught mom who has lost both of her teenage daughters' hearts to the world due to their

---

9. Richard Arum and Josipa Roksa, *Academically Adrift*, Kindle Edition, Locations 1251-1256.

community college classes. One instructor is a feminist and has been telling the class not to listen to their parents and not to believe what they have said. It will take a miracle to recover those relationships.

Even if the course is advertised as "Christian," do your homework. One parent whose son attended a Christian college that is highly promoted in homeschool circles shared with us about the drinking and parties that went on there. They brought him home.

The Worst Reason

While this next section is a little off-topic for buying a house debt-free, perhaps we can tie it in. Sometimes young people want to go to college to "escape from their parents." Hopefully, if you have encouraged your son to begin a business, he has owned that vision and is already successful in it. For our family, that process built the parent and child relationships and strengthened them. Our hearts were knit even closer as we helped our sons get their businesses off the ground. They consulted with us, and we gave them advice.

That outcome isn't always the case. We live in a fallen world with imperfect people and thus we must at times deal with relationship issues as they occur. The primary responsibility of fathers is to bring up their children in the nurture and admonition of the Lord. "And, ye fathers, provoke not your children to wrath: but bring them up in the nurture and admonition of the Lord" (Ephesians 6:4). As dads endeavor to disciple their sons, there is the possibility that a son will react negatively, straining the relationship. Notice that Ephesians 6:4 begins with a warning to fathers. We think the warning is there because if we provoke our children to anger, we won't have the relationship with them that is required to disciple them.

Our experience has taught us that if we have conflict, separation distances hearts not heals them. Humility, love, and submission are what is required for both the father and the son. "Submitting yourselves one to another in the fear of God" (Ephesians 5:21). If there aren't clear consciences, it will be extremely difficult to hear God's still small voice. Even if you have been praying about your son going to college, don't expect a sure word from the Lord until offenses are dealt with.

Once there is peace and restoration, then seek the Lord for guidance regarding college. It is likely the pressure to go will have been mitigated. "And we know that all things work together for good to them that love God, to them who are the called according to *his* purpose" (Romans 8:28). God is so merciful and desires His best for our lives, but we must meet His conditions. Resolve difficulties with your children quickly, or they will bear bad fruit.

Come to Your Conclusion

Because of the value you place on your children, we plead with you to critically read this chapter without bias (and maybe even reread it several times). We suggest you read the two books we have referred to—*Academically Adrift* and *College Unbound*.

We believe you will come away challenging the myth of "college for everyone." Talk to young people who have recently graduated from college and entered, or attempted to enter, the workforce. How long did it take them to graduate? Do they have school debt? Do they have the job and pay they were expecting? Do they still walk with the Lord?

College is a costly and time-consuming proposition. In addition, the faith of many is undermined during their higher-education years. This time in our sons' lives is extremely valuable. They can use those years to establish themselves in a business while saving money to purchase a home. We want you to question the usual conclusion that young people should go to college. We hope that we have given you the negative perspective of that direction and set before you other possibilities.

Chapter 10 Questions

- Have you planned on your son attending college and have you saved to help him?
- What is the reasoning behind the decision for him to attend college?
- What would his lost income be if he attended college?
- How would college be paid for? Is borrowing an option?
- Is getting the degree predicated on finding a good paying job?
- Have you considered the potential impact on his faith?
- Is it possible college is being used as an escape from home? If so, how can you fix the problem?

- If you are still considering college, are you willing to read *Academically Adrift: Limited Learning on College Campuses* by Richard Arum and Josipa Roksa, and *College Unbound: The Future of Higher Education and What It Means for Students* by Jeffrey J. Selingo?

11 ENTREPRENEUR OR EMPLOYEE?

Jacob, now 24 years old, has had a towing business since he was 20. He is a volunteer first responder for the local fire department and the volunteer town constable. Jacob is blessed with a dad who is an excellent role model in living debt-free, and thus it is the only way of life Jacob knows.

One day Jacob heard about a 1.6-acre property with a three-bedroom, 2 ½-bath house, a shop, and 20 storage units on it. Next to it was a 20-acre property that was not salable. It had previously been a pallet factory and was covered with stacks of rejected pallets. The bank was stuck with both properties until the 20-acre lot could be cleaned up and made attractive to a buyer. The bank had one offer from a contractor to do the work for $250,000.

Jacob's dad suggested Jacob make a proposal to the bank that he would clean up the 20-acre parcel in exchange for the 1.6 acre lot next to it. Jacob would be receiving a debt-free house including rentable storage units in exchange for his labor. The bank would be saving $250,000 in contractor fees and have a 20-acre salable lot. They accepted the proposal.

Jacob applied for and was granted a special permit required to burn processed wood. In accordance with county regulations, he couldn't burn any time the wind was greater than 10 miles per hour. Jacob also needed a unique piece of equipment, which in essence was a huge blower, to burn the pallets at a high temperature and reduce emissions into the environment. He and his dad were able to locate the machine and purchase it at a reasonable price. Jacob leased a loader to place the stacks of pallets into the family-owned dump truck so they could be moved to the burn pit.

It took six months to clean the land. Often Jacob would get up early to take advantage of the light winds typical at that time of day. He wasn't able to work every day because of weather conditions.

In addition to learning patience as he worked around the weather, Jacob became an expert at repairing large truck tires. The property was riddled with nails, and that meant flat tires. Jacob couldn't call out a repair service every time he experienced a flat tire on his equipment because of the expense. He had observed men in tire shops repairing tires so he decided to purchase the necessary tools and attempt the tire repairs himself. That first tire took quite a while, but after six months of fixing tires, he became efficient at it! Buying a house debt-free is a journey, and you never know what you are going to learn in the process.

Jacob now has his house whose estimated value is $275,000. He also owns those 20 storage units and will begin renting them soon. Jacob is an example of ingenuity, initiative, and hard work. The bank was so satisfied with Jacob's work that they had two more projects for him.

In this story of a debt-free house, we see the creativity of Jacob investing in equipment that would enable the work-for-trade agreement with the bank, which gave Jacob a house, 1.6 acres, plus 20 storage units. This obviously is the beginning of a profitable business for Jacob to pursue if he so desires.

The Entrepreneurial Spirit

If our sons are to avoid going to college, they will either be employees or have an entrepreneurial mindset. Let's start with the entrepreneurs. Many refer to an entrepreneur as someone who owns his own business, but according to the late Peter Drucker, the father of business management, an entrepreneur is someone who searches for change, responds to it, and exploits it as an opportunity. Google, Apple, Amazon, and Zappos are excellent examples of large-scale entrepreneurship in action.

Lest one be concerned that no more opportunities exist in regular businesses where there are many competitors, here is a good example. In the mid 1980s, Jerry and Janie Murrell had a deal for their four sons: Go to college or start a business. The Murrell brothers wisely decided they would open a business. In 1986, the brothers started a carry-out burger joint in Arlington, Virginia.

How could anyone hope to succeed in another fast-food burger restaurant with all the competition? They not only did well but were voted the number one burger restaurant in the Washington, D.C. area in spite of the competition. During the 1980s and 90s they continued to perfect their burgers and process. Then in 2003, they began offering franchises around the country. A July 18, 2012, *Forbes* article reports their sales as $950 million. You know them as Five Guys Burgers, and they have grown over 792% since 2006. Five Guys is currently the fastest growing restaurant chain. By the way, in case you noticed and wondered how they went from four brothers to five guys, the original five were the four brothers plus Dad. Later, the five guys were the four brothers plus another younger brother who decided to join the company.

Your Son's Business

Ideally your son started a business in his teens that will take him into his early 20s and beyond. All of our sons started working by doing lawn maintenance. It was a business that required relatively low capital. They were also able to develop business skills such as marketing, customer service, billing, and bookkeeping. While that business can be a life-long vocation for some, it was not what our boys wanted to pursue. By their early 20s, four of our five sons had their own business endeavors, and as previously stated, three of them already have purchased their houses debt-free before they were 30. Our fifth son, who is the youngest and still only 19, works for two of his brothers while developing his vocational skills. The goal is that in time, Lord willing, they would each have their own profit centers, customer base, and a business that can be passed on to their children. They aren't rich, but they make a very livable income and are debt-free. If Nathan or Christopher wants to take a day off to go to the zoo with their children, they can take it. They control their schedules and income. If they feel God leading in a new direction, they are free to change course.

What Business?

A portion of a chapter is not sufficient to fully cover the topic of self-employment. We could say so much about starting and owning one's own business, but for the present we will have to settle for the highlights and then how they apply to buying a house debt-free.

The temptation is to ask, "What business can my son have?" Without the path mapped out before us, we might feel uncomfortable and doubt whether it is possible. We live in the land of great opportunity, however. There is no limit to what we can do when we apply ourselves. The goal is not the pursuit of money, but to provide for a future family in a reasonable amount of time, as one serves the Lord.

We all seem to prefer 10 easy steps or formulas; however, we haven't found life in Christ to be like that. "Trust in the LORD with all thine heart; and lean not unto thine own understanding. In all thy ways acknowledge him, and he shall direct thy paths" (Proverbs 3:5-6). The source and quantity of your son's income from his own business will be determined largely by the decisions that have been and will be made in his life. If he is a man of virtue who is depending on the Lord Jesus Christ, a diligent worker, a resourceful person, and a lifelong learner, we believe he will do well.

When your son owns his business you are reaping the fruit of the hard work of raising a responsible man of God. If your son doesn't go to college he has a four year or more jumpstart over others who do so in establishing a business and saving money toward buying a house. Wouldn't that be exciting?

Our Personal Experience

When our sons were in their early teens, none of them knew the direction the Lord would take him. At that age, though, they had a mindset to learn skills and try whatever opportunities were presented to them. Before Nathan, our oldest son, graduated from high school, we had him research and then take steps to set up a corporation. We wanted the legal aspects in place for our sons to be self-employed.

ENTREPRENEUR OR EMPLOYEE?

We have shared some of Nathan's and Christopher's stories toward this end in the earlier chapters. Nathan volunteered his computer skills in publishing our homeschool support group's newsletter. That led to his teaching job and then on to a position in Steve's place of employment. Those skills gave him the offer of a full-time, well-paid job. Eventually, that led to Nathan working independently in our family's corporation. That family corporation has provided an umbrella for each of the boys to work under to help keep overhead costs low and minimize the time involved in government legalities such as taxes and workers' compensation. Within that corporation, each son has his own profit center.

How much do the boys value being independently self-employed? It is common for them to have employment offers from those for whom they are working or from others who know of their skills. They turn them down. Recently, one of the boys had a job offer in another state for over $100,000 a year. With his business growing, however, this son sees his future potential, not only for income but also for independence in self-employment, as being of far greater value than a near-term large salary.

Let's recall Mark from chapters 1 and 2, Joshua from chapter 7, Eric from chapter 8, Brad from chapter 10, and Jacob above. They were looking for opportunities and applying themselves. They were learning what it takes to conduct a business. Once someone gets over the initial feeling of not knowing what to do and simply starts doing something, he has made a huge step forward.

Looking for Opportunities

When we were growing up, we remember Sears catalog shopping throughout the year. Then came the special Wish Book Christmas edition. Each member of the family would take his turn scouring its pages for just the right Christmas gift purchase. We haven't seen one of those catalogs in years and understand they are no longer shipping them any more because of the shift to ordering online. Times change. When one door closes, several more open.

Who would have considered shopping for everything from toothpaste to tools or books to baking powder online? Who would have thought of ordering shoes that you have not tried on? We want to encourage you that as you and your son seek the Lord for His direction for your son's future entrepreneurial endeavors, the Lord will direct. He will open and close doors. But it is vitally important that your son's heart remains first and foremost focused on his relationship with Jesus Christ and serving Him. "All these things shall be added unto you" comes from those right priorities.

Steve has men contact him regularly asking his counsel concerning starting a business or an employment opportunity. As he begins to question them concerning their time in the Word and their relationship with Christ, it soon becomes obvious why some of them are seeking his input: They are not in God's Word.

We have found that generally a person's desire for the Word of God daily is indicative of their walk with the Lord. It's similar to a couple who does not desire to spend daily time together. Their communication will not be what it is when they are spending quality time with each other every day. In a similar fashion, when someone isn't in the Word on a daily basis, he is less likely to be able to clearly hear the Lord's still small voice. We want to be in a place where we can hear God's direction and follow it.

Employment Versus Self-Employment

Marketable skills can be used either in obtaining a job or in running a business. We have shared examples of men who purchased their homes debt-free using both avenues. While we want to encourage you to motivate your son to start his own business, some will prefer to work for another. Compare the advantages and disadvantages of employment and self-employment on the next page.

Employment	
Advantages	Disadvantages
Generally steady income	Layoffs are common today
Vacation	Vacation when approved
Healthcare	Employee-shared portion will rise
Retirement options	Pensions declining
Problems are ultimately management's	Suffer from others' bad decisions
Narrow skill-set required	Poor transferability to other jobs
Fewer personal decisions	Dictated schedule
Promotion opportunities	Advancement may be difficult
Guaranteed retirement pension if you meet company's requirements	Cash only inheritance
Degree may be the ticket	Income may not compensate for degree
Corporate decreed policies	May be unbiblical
	Can't control environment (bad language, ungodly music, etc.)

Self-Employment	
Advantages	Disadvantages
No limit to income potential	Owner can be financially liable
Vacation as desired	May not be able to take off
Can choose healthcare coverage	Healthcare expense might be a significant percentage of sales dollars
Owner's decision on retirement	Dependent on company success
Able to solve problems	May have to go outside for problem resolution
No limits to using skills	May have less time to acquire skills
Able to make all decisions	More decisions than desired
No limits to success potential	Can be difficult to control time invested
The business can be an inheritance	Children may not want it
No degree required	

A Livable Wage

It is important that our sons earn a livable wage if they desire that their wives not work and be available to homeschool their children. Also the more hours he must work to provide for the family, the less time he has to spend with them. With a debt-free home, he can live on at least 25% less income than others. If he chooses employment, there are types of jobs that tend to have higher incomes. The more people there are who are willing and able to perform a job, then the law of supply and demand will drive that wage down. Jobs that pay a premium wage are likely going to involve one or more of the following:

- Shortage of manpower. Two examples are the various military conflicts overseas that have created high-priced contractor positions in those regions and U.S. oil fields in Alaska and the Dakotas that have done the same.

- Undesirable hours, whether long or inconvenient, or long periods of separation. The worse the hours, generally the fewer who will work them and the higher the pay to recruit workers.

- Hazardous. No matter how dangerous a job may be, there is a threshold that will induce men to work in those conditions.

- Above-average knowledge or experience. Through the ages, it was gained by study, apprenticeship, and the school of "hard knocks."

Clearly, from a family-favored perspective, the last point is the most desirable. As we discussed earlier, being an autodidact is important to staying ahead of the learning curve. Encourage your son to plan a slice of time into his daily schedule for continuous self-improvement.

What Will He Do?

Employment or self-employment are options for young men to provide for their families. We want to encourage your sons toward self-employment. Our sons have been blessed with self-employment and have avoided the influences so many others struggle with when employed. They have also earned good wages facilitating their house savings. As each entered his prime income-producing years after high school, we really didn't know how he would earn money, except we knew college was not in his future. As we look back, we can see how God directed their study and experience. They weren't idle but always growing and learning as you can see from reading their various stories.

We think as you and your son seek the Lord, he will find what the Lord has for his vocation, just as our sons did. We hope your son will be directed to begin his own business. Ideally it will be a successful venture that can facilitate saving for a house debt-free before the expense of supporting a family becomes a part of his life.

If your son feels led to work for someone else, he needs to consider several points as he makes that decision. He needs an income and a future that will allow him to support his family. Before he has a family, his income should be such that he can be saving well toward purchasing his home debt-free. That will be an indication of how feasible it is to live off that salary with a family.

Whether an entrepreneur or an employee, our son's first priority is seeking the Lord and His righteousness. As he does that, the Lord indicates that He will take care of his needs. We believe these are exciting spiritual lessons for our children to be learning, and we want them to have these kinds of opportunities.

Chapter 11 Questions

- What are your son's interests?
- What are potential businesses for your son?
- Has he committed to focused prayer and fasting for venture ideas?
- How can you encourage your son to develop business skills?

12 WHEN THE MOMENT ARRIVES!

Justin will be turning 21 in a short time. He is quite young to own his house debt-free. His story is unique, yet similar to the others. He has been married for almost a year, and he and his wife are expecting their first child. He humbly gives God every bit of the glory for all He has done in his life. He says he is a work in progress as we all should be.

Justin was blessed to grow up with parents who love the Lord Jesus, where family is important, and where they have a good work ethic. He has five brothers and one sister.

Some may remember the ad many years ago in the back of *Popular Mechanics* magazine to purchase your own sawmill. Five years before Justin was born, Justin's dad bought a sawmill similar to that one.

Most young men have a fascination with equipment, and when Justin, at 14 years old, took an interest in the sawmill his dad taught him how to use it. Justin did contract sawing for others and became quite experienced sawing lumber.

Also when Justin was 14, a mutual friend introduced his family to a family from Texas. Justin and a son from the other family became good friends even though they lived almost 900 miles apart.

At one point, Justin wrestled with whether he should go to college and get a traditional job with a company. As he prayed, he felt God telling him to minister to his family and entrust the future to Him. For Justin, this was seeking first the kingdom of God. Sometimes he did local construction work, but for the most part he helped his family.

At 18, Justin was invited to do contract highway labor for a family in Texas. A side blessing to this work was that Justin spent the weekends with his friend's family. As the Lord often uses situations like these, Justin became interested in his friend's sister. It didn't take too long before they began courting.

So, engaged and anticipating marriage, 18-year-old Justin began thinking about the need for a place to live. He had approximately $2,500 to his name from his previous construction projects, and that wouldn't buy or build a house.

Justin had always admired well-constructed log homes, and for about a year he had been thinking that he would like to build a dovetail log home of his own. He discussed it with his dad, who offered to let him use the family tractor, sawmill, tools, and any other equipment he might need. His family owns 137 acres, mostly covered in trees, and his dad also said he could have all the trees he needed for his house. Justin's family agreed to sell him a parcel of property on which to build his house. Justin had a plan.

In January, Justin began logging and then sawing the logs into lumber. He worked until May when he ran out of money. Even though the logs were free, he spent his savings on fuel and equipment repairs. To rebuild his savings, in May he worked construction and then sawed until the end of September when he had again depleted his savings.

His future in-laws had a business making vintage-style doll furniture beds. The dad's other company was consuming too much of his time to keep up with the furniture orders. They offered Justin the opportunity to take over making the doll furniture. Here was a good reason to spend time with his fiancé while earning some more money. He spent the remainder of the year with her family making furniture.

When Justin had another $6,000, he estimated that he had just enough to complete his house. On New Year's Day, he went back home to begin building. It took him three months to make his home livable, and on March 30, their wedding day, they moved in. It is still fairly rustic, but they are very happy in their house.

Justin's home has two stories, with one bathroom, and is 2,000 square feet. It has electricity but just barely some running water. Justin continues to finish the house as they rejoice in God's mercy and grace in their lives. He gives God the glory for all that others did in volunteering and helping him with his house.

Don't ever tell Justin he won't be able to do something that he knows God has called him to do. I'm confident he will smile, turn to look at his wife's smile, cast a glance around his debt-free home, and likely respond with, "God hasn't failed me yet, so I don't anticipate that He will in the future." We ask you, what is that worth?

Is It Time?

The stories we have shared with you generally have a common thread. No clear decision point indicated when it was time to buy or build. That is why having a son who is trusting the Lord to guide him is the most important aspect of his life. There is no formula for that. When does he know he has saved enough? When is it the right house and circumstances? Should he always be looking for a house? Should he settle for one that needs a great deal of work or that is in a less-desirable location?

Once a young man starts actively looking to purchase a home, he often finds it difficult to rest, work, save, and wait on the Lord. You have probably observed this in your own experience.

Encourage your son to prayerfully set a savings goal for his house that is realistic for the area in which he is interested in raising a family. Then suggest he "go to sleep" to the idea of actually purchasing his house with an agreed-upon savings goal being his alarm clock. When the alarm goes off, he wakes up and checks the time. Depending on circumstances, he will either get up to begin his house search or snooze for a while longer. The primary job during this season is saving and acquiring skills. Although God may bring something before he hits the goal, this mindset will give peace in the meantime.

For our area, $100,000 is a low number for a reasonable house, but it's the number we have in our minds. Christopher and Joseph had more than that in savings when they purchased their homes, and Nathan had less.

Reviewing the Stories

Nathan wasn't looking for a house when the neighbor approached him asking if he wanted to buy his mother's house. Even though Nathan didn't have all the money in hand for the house purchase, he was at peace knowing that God was leading him to get it and that God would provide. Christopher also had a neighbor approach him about buying a house. After prayer, Christopher knew the first house wasn't the Lord's best, and the second house, which was our house, was the right one even though it cost more than the first house he was offered. Jacob pursued the pallet cleanup job when it seemed like a far-fetched proposal. Ben didn't have enough money to buy a house, but the Lord led him to build a house with his dad. After that, he had enough for his house.

Once Eric had his real estate broker's license, he kept his eyes open for a house that he could afford and that would meet his future needs. In time God led him to one that was a great value. Ryan patiently looked for a long time. He waited on the Lord until he knew it was just the right house. Waiting on the Lord and not getting ahead of Him is key. Justin was in a courtship and knew that he would soon have need for a house.

You probably have great practical experience to share with your son concerning actually buying a house when he gets to that point. We would also like to touch on a few of the highlights of this process.

Counting the Cost of Ownership

Prepare your son for the surprising number of bills he can expect once he closes on his home. As homeowners, you know there are property taxes, gas and electric utilities, telephone, insurance, upkeep, possibly housing association dues, and perhaps monitoring for a security system. It is unlikely that your son is familiar with these expenses unless you have been working with him on family budgeting and discussing the costs of home ownership.

If your son isn't living in his house, his utilities will be lower, but the minimums will still need to be paid. If he isn't living in the house, his insurance likely will be double or higher than what it would normally be to insure the house because the house is vacant.

One must be prepared for the monthly bills that come with home ownership. If the house needs work, there is no easier time to accomplish it than when it is unoccupied. Encourage your son to lay all these factors before the Lord seeking His guidance when he is seriously considering a house purchase.

Where Should He Buy?

It is wise to help our sons consider carefully where they will purchase a house. For example, we live over three miles from a railroad track that runs along the Missouri River. Would you believe that when we have a window cracked slightly, we can hear the coal trains as they blow their horns passing through town several times during the night? They don't bother us much, but what if those tracks were closer and someone was a light sleeper?

When Steve was growing up, he lived in a residential area about a half mile from a processing plant for a well-known brand of lunch meats. When the wind was blowing the right direction, the smell was terrible. His family didn't live there very long. The economical price of their house brought them to the neighborhood, but the smell drove them away.

Who likes the sound of barking dogs when trying to sleep? People will sell and move to get away from it. Ever heard someone tell about an obnoxious neighbor or one who has been in prison for a crime that requires notifying neighbors? The neighborhood could have a high crime rate. Maybe a neighbor drives loud motorcycles or cars.

Evaluating the House

Here are some questions to consider when evaluating a possible house purchase:

- How likely is your son to be able to sell it for at least what he paid for it?
- If the house needs to be improved will he be able to get all of his money back?
- Is the house better or worse than the others in the neighborhood?
- Does the foundation have structural issues?
- Does the basement flood?
- Is there mold or high levels of radon gas in the house?
- Is it located near high-voltage power lines?
- Is there a marshy, mosquito breeding ground nearby?
- Is the house in a flood plain?
- Is it a neighborhood in which your son will feel his wife would be safe when he isn't home?
- What about raising children there?
- Is there water nearby that could present a danger to small children?
- What are the zoning laws of the neighborhood?
- Could a manufacturing plant be built next door?
- Are there plans for widening a road or building a bypass near the property?

The answers to all of these questions could significantly impact the house's value and your son's future in it should he buy it.

Why Is It a Good Deal?

When money is a consideration, we often like to think "cheap." There are going to be less expensive houses in areas where people are less inclined to live. Often people have good reasons for selling houses for low prices. Find out why a particular house is inexpensive, and confirm it with neighbors and a real-estate agent.

Seldom is a neighborhood "perfect," but before your son buys a house, he should be aware of any issues there may be in that neighborhood. If he doesn't know the neighborhood, encourage your son to spend time there, especially evenings. He can park in the street, watch, and listen. Have him observe both from in front of the house and from the street behind the house, since that house will be his backyard neighbors. He might even want to talk with the neighbors. Information he gathers in this way can be invaluable as he considers making an offer on the house.

Building

Building his own home is an option for your son to consider if he has experience with the trades. That is one advantage to your son learning those skills. Sometimes one can get good deals on property because land tends to sell more slowly than houses. There are, however, some challenges to consider with building.

Building requires a significant investment of time. Before making that decision, your son will want to be sure both he has the time available and that he is willing to use his time in that way.

From our experience, we have found that even if you are a good negotiator, a self-builder will not get the same pricing from contractors and supply companies that an established builder receives. Plus, unforeseen things will come along that keep driving the cost up. He should expect his final costs to be higher than his pre-building estimates. Be especially wary of dollar-per-square-foot estimates since building costs vary widely based on the quality of construction and finish options.

Building Codes

It is important that your son research governing laws and building codes prior to deciding to build. An F5 tornado ripped through the town of Joplin, Missouri, on May 22, 2011. It was the costliest single tornado in U.S. history and the deadliest since 1947. As a result, the NIST Engineering Laboratory has proposed more stringent building codes. Communities can adopt any building codes they choose, and the more rigorous they are, the higher the cost to build. For instance, as of January 1, 2011, California requires residential fire sprinklers. Future building codes will likely make new construction more costly than houses built under previous code.

Your son should determine what governing authority a proposed property would be under and then what the cost would be to build to that code. Your son can visit the local governing office to get a list of the applicable codes. We have had a fantastic experience working with our local code enforcement department. We have spoken with others who have built their homes and found their local office was antagonistic to self-builders. Don't expect the city inspectors to educate your son. It is reasonable, though, that they inform him of the governing law. Keep in mind that these codes can be your friend whether building or buying because they provide guidance for quality construction.

One way to understand the effect of codes on the final price is to discuss the proposed venture with an experienced builder. We caution you to be upfront with him about your son's interest in building. Respect the builder's time and don't waste it if there is no likelihood of using him. One option, though, would be for the builder to frame the house in and leave the rest of the finishing to your son. That is what we did when we built our house. Even though some builders will not be interested in a partial job like that, others may be. Prior to signing a contract, strongly encourage your son to speak to people who have had that contractor build their homes.

A Unique Opportunity

Jim Bob Duggar suggested another possibility for young men to consider. First buy a piece of property. Then wait to find a house that is going to be torn down and offer to move the house. Properties are sometimes being sold for use as commercial purposes or there is a new road going in or one being widened.

They will tear down perfectly good houses to make room for new construction. Perhaps even an older house will be demolished so that a new one can be built in its place. If you move the house, it will save the owner the cost of demolition, and you will have a house to put on your property.

Years ago, Jim Bob did just that. He purchased a piece of property. Then he heard of a building he could move inexpensively and put on his property. When he sold the property a few years later, he made a very handsome profit.

The Fixer Upper

If your son doesn't have the time to build a house, he might get a good deal on a "fixer-upper" home or "handyman's special." Even if he doesn't have construction skills, working on his own home will be a good way to learn them. Bill in chapter 6 was able to buy a house very inexpensively because it didn't have a bathtub in it. It is likely the house needed other work as well.

With a fixer-upper house, you can sometimes buy in a nicer neighborhood than you could have otherwise afforded because the price is lower due to its disrepair. If the purchase takes all the money your son has available, he can do the remodeling over time as he earns more funds.

Joseph, our third son, whose story comes in the last chapter, bought a house that needed updating. He had the money available to do that work because the house cost less than what he had saved. With no immediate need to live in the house, he spent the next two years working on the remodel, which was only a three-minute drive from our house.

The Prayerful Decision

A friend who is very wise in real estate matters says that you make your money on a house when you buy it not when you sell it. This indicates the importance of waiting on the Lord and not becoming impatient.

Your son must consider many factors before making an offer on a particular house. Your personal house-buying experience can help your son as he navigates through those factors. With this information, your son can make a prayerful, reasonable decision. The more he knows about the home, the better his decision-making capabilities will be when weighing the pros and cons of the home.

It is possible that the decision might be made to purchase property and build a house rather than buy an existing home. There is much to research and consider before finalizing that decision.

Without the pressure of immediate need, your son has the opportunity to look, pray, and think. He can pass up "so-so" choices and wait for the one that is stunning. Prayer and family discussions can help him as he makes those decisions. They are critical. To save for a debt-free home and then to be disappointed in the actual home is not the outcome we want for our sons. May we encourage our sons to do research, be patient, and seek the Lord.

Chapter 12 Questions

- How can you help your son be asleep to buying a home and to wait on the Lord to wake him up?

- What would the dollar amount be for the alarm?

- What anticipated expenses will there be once your son owns his home? Help him list them.

- Based on your son's finances and trade skills, is either building or fixing up a home an option? Why?

- If your son is interested in building or fixing a home up, how can he investigate the building codes?

- What things should your son consider before a house purchase? Help him make a list of them.

13 THE CASH BUYER

Tyler is the second oldest son out of five, and he has one sister. His dad was a database developer but desired a family business where he could work with his family. Therefore as he continued his job, his family began operating a bakery with the hopes of growing it large enough to allow him to quit his job.

At 17, Tyler began working part-time for the bakery while he finished his last year of high school. After graduating he worked full-time in the bakery. By then, his father had left his job to grow the bakery business. It became evident, though, that the bakery wouldn't support the family sufficiently, and so his dad again found a job in the city. Tyler was content to invest his time in the family business with the goal of having it produce significant income in the future.

BUYING A HOUSE DEBT-FREE

When Tyler was 21, his parents began to discuss how their two sons, who were both working full-time in the bakery, would be able to support families. They decided to abandon the bakery in pursuit of better income potential. They purchased two fixer-upper houses to refurbish and then resell. The sons would do the work and earn the income from the projects. Dad used family savings to buy the houses, but the sons would share the profit. Temporarily supplying cash to purchase the houses was one way the dad felt the family could repay a portion of the investment the sons had made in the bakery business.

It took six months to refurbish both houses and sell them. First, the boys paid their dad back. Then each son's share was about $7,000 from the first house and $20,000 on the second. Tyler used some of the proceeds to purchase a truck and a few other things he needed, bringing his savings down to $25,000.

Since real estate values were quite low in their area, Tyler was confident of finding a fixer-upper house in his price range with the cash he had available. It took a month of looking before he purchased his $19,000 house. It is a good starter home with two bedrooms, one bath, and 1,100 square feet on one acre. At 23, Tyler owns his home debt-free.

The next phase of Tyler's life is skill and income enhancement. If he hadn't been ready to buy a house of his own, he could have taken his profit and invested it in another house to remodel and resell, with a goal of making more on each house he turned around. He currently has an entry-level marketing position and is learning more with the goal of advancement.

Cash Equals Quick Sale

In the housing market, cash usually means a fast, sure sale. Mortgage paperwork and inspections can delay a closing or cause the deal to fall through. A mortgage often requires a termite inspection and a house appraisal. If inspections find problems, it is generally the seller's responsibility to fix things, but that can be negotiable. If the house appraises for less than the selling price, then either the deal fails, or the buyer has to come up with the difference between what the bank will loan and the sale price. It can be worth it to the seller to take less money for a sure sale than to hope he will incur no surprises with mortgage-company approval. If a mortgage is involved and the house-selling price is greater than the appraised value, then the seller must take the appraisal value. If the seller won't accept the lower price, then the contract is terminated, and the search for a new buyer begins. A cash offer avoids this situation and will appeal to many sellers.

When negotiating for a better price, do it with Christ-like conduct. There are ways of negotiating that don't bring in an antagonistic spirit. Statements such as: "You may be able to get more from someone else, but I feel I can only offer …" or "With my other budget considerations, all I can offer is …" and then, "I fully understand if you don't feel comfortable in accepting my offer. Take a few days to consider it, but I will continue to look for a house in the meantime. If you change your mind and I haven't found one, then we can do business."

We've seen professing Christians who are ruthless negotiators. Scripture tells us, "And whatsoever ye do in word or deed, *do* all in the name of the Lord Jesus, giving thanks to God and the Father by him" (Colossians 3:17). We doubt that a seller who just had a negative bargaining encounter with a professing Christian would be interested in hearing about the Lord Jesus.

A cash sale can also be desirable to the seller because it offers a quick closing. As little as two weeks will still allow sufficient time for a title search and home inspection.

For both Joseph and Bill, the seller was motivated to accept the offer based on the prospect of cash in hand. Joseph's house had been on the market the year before, taken off for several months, and had reappeared. Even though Joseph's cash offer was considerably less than the asking price, it was a sure sale. The agent encouraged her client to accept the offer.

Since Bill's house wasn't complete, it would not have qualified for a mortgage, and cash was the only way it could be sold. The bank could have hired someone to finish the bathroom, enabling it to be sold conventionally, but the Lord alone knows why they chose not to do that. Truly it was Bill's blessing that it was sold as-is.

Home Inspection

We consulted with Eric, the young agent from chapter 8, on this chapter. One point he felt strongly about is the importance of getting a home inspection. In his experience he has seen a few homes where the inspection revealed huge "money traps." He felt the $300 or so a prospective buyer pays for a home inspection is nothing compared to the costs a buyer could incur if problems surfaced later.

When friends of ours tried to sell their condominium in Connecticut, a pre-sale inspection determined that the loft and fireplace had not had building permits when installed. The people from whom our friends had purchased the condo added the loft and fireplace. They should have obtained permits before performing the work because it was not part of the original construction.

Our friends had to remove the drywall around the fireplace and the loft so a building inspector could inspect. The fireplace turned out to be okay, but the loft needed work to satisfy the building inspector, so they had to hire someone to do the work. Had our friends paid for a home inspection prior to purchasing the home, these issues would have surfaced and been resolved before they bought the condo saving them money and headaches. They would not have been the ones dealing with problems when they wanted to sell.

For Sale By Owner

For Sale by Owner (FSBO) is a viable option for your son in his home purchase. That is what Nathan did when he was offered his house and what Christopher did when he bought our house. We have personally purchased two houses and sold two without using real estate agents. There are greater risks in that approach, and you aren't guaranteed a better deal.

A FSBO house has the potential of selling for less money because the real estate agents' commissions are not included in the asking price. It is possible, maybe even likely, that the seller is asking the same price he would have listed for with an agent, and then he intends to pocket the amount that would have been paid out in commissions. Therefore, the buyer needs to do research on the value of the house and any potential problems. There could be a host of issues that only someone with experience may discover, and that could be why the seller is avoiding using a real estate agent.

It may be that your son wants to hire an appraiser and a home inspector once he is fairly certain of the house. With appraisal fees around $500 and home inspection around $300, he will want to be sure this is his choice of a house before he invests some of his savings on these services.

Forsalebyowner.com is a website that your son can visit when he is actively looking for a house to buy to see what is available in the area in which he wants to purchase. Not all FSBO homes will be listed, but many likely will be. Fewer people will be looking at these houses compared to those on the Multiple Listing Service (MLS) that agents use and comb.

Your son should also consider the services of a real estate attorney in obtaining and reviewing a FSBO contract. When we sold our house to Christopher, we called the closing company and asked them to e-mail us a blank contract that would be applicable in Kansas. Though lawyers can be expensive, even more so are legal problems that can arise in our litigious society. Proceed with great caution if buying a FSBO house and seek legal counsel as appropriate.

A Good Real Estate Agent

If an agent is offering the house, your son will need to use an agent to tour the house and eventually make an offer. If he uses the seller's agent, beware as that agent is representing the seller's best interests.

It seems that everyone knows someone who is a real estate agent. When you receive a recommendation, ask if the one making the recommendation has purchased or sold a house using him. Just because he is a friend or someone who goes to the referrer's church isn't good enough. Has the one referring used the agent's professional services? Was the agent responsive and motivated? Was he knowledgeable about neighborhoods, property values, and state laws? Was he pleasant and ethical?

The agent can do a comparative market analysis (CMA) to ballpark the value of the house. You might be comfortable enough with that to forgo a $500 appraisal. If your son has been working with an agent and a FSBO home becomes of interest, it is not uncommon that FSBO houses will offer some commission to the buyer's agent. Then you might be able to save on the listing commission and still have the benefit of an experienced agent. Encourage your son to do as much research as he can possibly do on his own concerning the house purchase. That will also validate what the agent is telling him and he will earn credibility with him, diminishing the possibility of his being taken advantage of in the purchase. Of course, dealing with someone with extensive real estate experience is not a guarantee you won't end up with unexpected problems, but it should help.

Buying a Short Sale or Foreclosure

If your son were to buy a "short sale" or foreclosed home, it could potentially save him money, but the risks can be significant as mentioned in the previous section, especially on a foreclosed home. A short sale occurs when the seller realizes that the house is worth less in the current market than the amount currently owed on the mortgage and wants out. To sell the house, the lender must agree to take the loss, and that process can take months and at times over a year. If there is a second mortgage, a difficult purchase can now be much more so.

Foreclosure occurs when the homeowner has failed to make his committed payments, and the bank has legally repossessed the home. The home may have been empty for months. Often the house is in a state of disrepair and has suffered much abuse. If the homeowner didn't have money to make the payments, you can be sure he wasn't doing necessary maintenance.

Steve once saw a Craigslist ad where everything inside the empty home was for sale. Solid oak doors, granite countertops, oak trim, expensive carpet, plumbing fixtures and appliances were being offered for pennies on the dollar. It was obvious the home was being foreclosed on, and the soon-to-be-replaced "owner" was getting all the cash out of the house he could. We are told this is not all that uncommon these days.

Foreclosed homes may be sold in a number of ways including sheriff's auctions. Our understanding is that an auction can be very risky because it generally does not allow for prior inspection of the house before placing a bid. Google: "should I buy a foreclosure or short sale" to research the advantages and disadvantages of either route. Then seek the advice of a trusted real estate agent. A great price on a distressed house may not be such a deal after all.

Closing Costs Are Lower with Cash

The closing costs will vary by region, because additional fees are generally required when financing with a mortgage versus when purchasing with cash. As mentioned above, with a mortgage there will normally be an appraisal and one or more inspections. There will be a loan origination fee, which can be significant. There may also be a mortgage tax. Some lenders may require a home warranty. If the seller doesn't include it in the package, the buyer will have to pay for it. Likely, money will be put in escrow for future tax liabilities on a mortgage closing. That isn't required when paying cash. Title insurance becomes an optional expense, and it should be lower if you are paying cash. Paying cash is the smart alternative.

Internet Research

Your son can do a great amount of house research on the Internet. Type in an address and usually in a second or two, you can view a picture of the house. Websites such as zillow.com, trulia.com, and realtor.com are helpful for researching neighborhood property values. Public record details such as square feet, number of bedrooms and baths, type of construction, type of heating, fireplaces, lot size, and property tax amount are generally available.

The Web can be used to find houses as they become available for sale through mls.com. Joseph saw the house he purchased on the day it was re-listed. He researched it and found that previously it had been offered for a while and then withdrawn. When it came up again, he contacted the listing agent immediately. The listing agent works for the seller's best interest. If the listing agent sells the house, however, he is receiving both the listing commission and the sales commission and has greater incentive to make the sale. The agent convinced the seller that a quick cash sale at the offered price was better than a higher price with a mortgage. Encourage your son to do as much research as he possibly can when he begins looking for his house.

To Move In or Not

A common question your son will hear once he has purchased a house is, "When are you moving in?" We've encountered that question from many, and some even appear to have an agenda of trying to pressure our sons into moving out of our home. The reality is that living at home with the family is still the cheapest way to live. Insurance on your son's house will be significantly lower if he lives in it, but the utilities and food costs will go up. Besides, our sons have greatly enjoyed the companionship of the family while living in our home. Living with your family also provides welcome accountability and less temptation. Our sons have found the decision to live at home until God gives them wives easy to make.

Should He Rent His House Temporarily?

Eric is renting out his home for $1,150 a month until he's married. Provided the tenants stay for several months, he will likely make a profit over what it will cost him to repair the house once they move out.

There are negatives to consider when renting out a house. Renters are notorious for doing damage to a property. Sometimes they fail to pay the rent, and it can be difficult to evict them. We have heard of touchy situations when renting to friends or fellow Christians.

It is important to run a credit check on anyone to whom your son is considering renting. Your son will need to be approved by a credit agency to run a check himself. Suggest that he Google "how to run a credit check on a tenant," and he will find the steps needed to do so. Some sites offer full background, criminal, eviction, and credit checks for $25–$30 a person.

Ezlandlordforms.com has state-specific forms that can be used if renting. He may be able to set up a direct deposit of the rent into his bank account eliminating late payments or the "check-is-in-the-mail" issues.

Your son must investigate the legal and tax ramifications of renting out his home. He will be paying income tax on the rental income, so he will need to research how to deduct expenses. He will still have to satisfy certain requirements. Most states have laws governing the amount of the security and damage deposits, how they are saved, whether interest must be paid on them, and what the deposits can be used for. Knowing the tax laws on rental income and costs ahead of time will save him grief later.

Our son Joseph decided not to rent his house. He had remodeled it to his specifications as a home he wanted to live in with a wife one day. The rental income wasn't worth the potential damage it might incur from renters.

As with all decisions, your son will want to pray and seek the Lord's guidance as to whether it is wise to rent his house until he needs to live in it. The Lord will continue to lead and give direction as He always has.

Buying Nitty Gritty

Cash tends to motivate sellers. The fact that your son has cash is a great negotiating lever. Use it to your son's advantage, and use it graciously as ambassadors for Christ.

Help your son determine whether he wants a real estate agent or attempts a FSBO negotiation. Finally, if your son buys his home before he is married, he will have to decide whether he will live in it, rent it, or continue living at home.

We know the excitement that occurs in a family on the day when a son is finally able to purchase his home debt-free. The years of praying, working, and saving have finally yielded a harvest. Whether it is a $19,000 house like Tyler purchased or a $210,000 house such as Christopher bought, the delight and potential of debt-free home ownership is very real. It is our prayer that each of your sons has this delightful experience to celebrate before he reaches 30.

Chapter 13 Questions

- What are advantages of buying with cash?
- What are the advantages of home inspections?
- What are the advantages of FSBO?
- Who might you recommend as a good real estate agent to your son? How has he proven himself a good agent?
- What are the advantages and disadvantages of buying a short sale or foreclosure? Would you encourage your son in this direction?

- Is your son still welcome to live in your home once he has purchased his own house?
- What are the advantages and disadvantages of your son renting out his house?

DISCLAIMER ** This chapter is provided as general information. Consider it as one friend discussing his experience with another. Nothing written herein shall be construed as legal advice. Seek appropriate legal and/or expert counsel as necessary. Ultimately, seek the direction of the Lord Jesus Christ and follow Him.

14 WHAT IF?

At age 18, Greg joined his father working for a Christian man doing construction. He started at $12 an hour and worked up to $20 by the time he turned 22. He saved all he could because years earlier he had read the book *Henry and the Great Society* by H.L. Roush, Sr., and it made a huge impression on him.

Henry was about a man who lived simply but was caught up with others in the desire to have things. Since Henry couldn't afford the things he wanted, he borrowed and became a slave to his debt. The book had a very sad ending. Greg decided he never wanted to be a slave to debt and would choose to live without conveniences if it meant becoming a slave to them.

Greg married at 23, and his wife shared his vision of looking to God to provide. They set up home in an apartment for one and a half years then purchased a small camper. They moved the camper to his parents' backyard and lived there for six months.

For two years, Greg had been looking for property to build a house on without success. His family had regularly ministered to an elderly widow neighbor, and Greg helped her with many projects for which she was very grateful. She had some land that Greg thought would be ideal, and she agreed to sell 20 acres for $78,000. Greg could almost have paid cash for it, but he would not have had anything left with which to build a house. They settled on $30,000 down with the rest in payments, without interest, to be paid off in a maximum of four years.

The day after they closed on the property, Greg moved the camper to the property and began building. He was able to build inexpensively because after he married, he purchased a sawmill and began sawing lumber for the house. He had stacked it so that it would be drying and ready for use once the Lord provided the land. Greg had also collected all the doors, some windows, sinks, and temporary cabinets through the years in preparation for building.

He first built a shed so he could store his tools securely out of the weather. Since it was October and winter came as early as November in their area, he worked hard and fast. By December they had an 1,100-square-foot home, with two bedrooms, one bath, and heat, courtesy of a wood stove. He had the foresight to cut and stack firewood previously, so that when he had a home the wood would be dry and ready to burn.

As you would expect from someone who plans ahead, this home was designed and built to be added on to. When God gives them children, they will be prepared to add on space, but until then this home is adequate.

The electric company wanted $10,000 to run power to their property so they have chosen to be off the grid for now. They have a 5,000 watt generator and battery bank to power their house, which is wired traditionally. They opted for a propane refrigerator to conserve energy because refrigerators draw much electricity. In time they will have utility power, but until then they are content.

Greg enjoys conveniences just like the rest of us, but he is committed to not being a slave to them. After our phone call, I told him I would send him a copy of his story and asked for his e-mail address. I think I detected a smile when he said he didn't have e-mail or even a computer. He said I could send it via snail mail. I think you can see how he earned a place in this book.

Some might wonder why Greg's story is included in a book on buying a house debt-free. It is here because we've had many tell us that in their area houses are too expensive to ever purchase debt-free, so they don't even try. Greg is a superb example to those who would want to give up or not start at all toward the goal of a debt-free house.

Greg's story involves a loan even though he didn't want to be a slave to debt. Did he miss God's best or God's timing? Only God knows the answer to that question. Whatever the case, we appreciated Greg's initiative, hard work, and preparation. Even though his story, like Bill's, was not debt-free "perfect," we included it because we felt it would be an encouragement to those with "what if" questions.

What If Houses in Our Area Cost Too Much?

Start now! We have heard many times that someone's son could never buy a house debt-free because they live in an area where housing prices are very high. No doubt that makes the goal more difficult, but it certainly is no reason not to give it one's best. It simply means that one has to work all the harder, smarter, and potentially longer to achieve the goal. There is no time to waste.

We received a note from someone in Australia. She said it was impossible to buy debt-free there because of how expensive even small homes are in her city. She told us how much her mortgage was and that by working hard she had decreased it greatly. Frankly, the amount she had paid her mortgage down in such a short amount of time was indicative that she could have paid cash for her home had she waited. If her parents hadn't let her live at home rent-free, or if they were in another city from her job and she had to rent a place to live, it would have likely taken much longer to save up the money. To further confirm the possibility that having money for a debt-free home might have been a choice, she said that if she hadn't borrowed she would not have been able to travel the world. The table from chapter 6 reminds us again of the number of weeks it would take to save

$100,000. Buying debt-free means we will forgo pleasures that others may feel are important or even necessary.

Remember Eric from chapter 8? Real estate in the Denver metro area is very expensive, and Eric had every reason to say he couldn't buy debt-free because of it. Instead, he started. He worked, saved, looked to the Lord, and was patient. The Lord provided Eric a house that is worth almost two times what he paid for it!

If your son starts and accumulates a good amount of savings, who knows what house deals the Lord may bring along for a cash buyer. We have discussed the leverage cash brings for a home that can't be mortgaged or is offered as a short sale. It might be a house that is up for auction or one that needs to be moved more quickly than the normal lending process would accommodate.

Perhaps the woman who will be your son's future wife has been a good steward of what she has been earning, and between the two of them they can buy their house debt-free.

Another consideration might be whether your family has the ability to resettle in a part of the country where the cost of living isn't so high. This would put all of your sons in a better position to purchase their homes debt-free and be more frugal for ongoing living expenses.

If the Lord is putting it on your son's heart to buy debt-free and nothing has come available for an affordable price, continue to wait. Seek the Lord. Fast and pray. In time, the Lord will make it clear.

In any case, your son will be much better off financially then he would be had he never had the goal of a debt-free house and instead chosen to spend his money as he made it.

What If He Wants to Get Married First?

Start now! Time is even more of the essence for a young man who is eager for marriage. Once a young man becomes interested in a young woman, it will be hard to delay marriage. This is similar to the difficulty of stopping or changing the course of an avalanche that has started rushing down a steep mountainside. The best approach is preemptive.

It's important that parents are encouraging their sons to be as financially established as possible while patiently waiting for the Lord to reveal His best for the son's future wife. "Trust in the LORD with all thine heart; and lean not unto thine own understanding" (Proverbs 3:5). This is a season of working hard, waiting, and preparing for marriage. It is a time for your family to make the most of the days remaining with your son before he establishes his own home.

Your ability to gently encourage your son to stay the course toward a debt-free house will be challenging if he is thinking of marriage before he has saved enough for the house. As you just read, Greg married before he had his home. He told us how the

Lord had led when he was younger to buy his house debt-free, and yet he didn't wait. Will he have regrets later?

If your son is feeling led to marry before he can buy a house, pray and fast with him to discern God's will clearly. Don't strive over it, however. Love him, support him, and don't pressure him to wait. Assuming he is over 20 years old, he is accountable to God as a man making his own decisions. There are many reasons why a debt-free home is a positive step to take before marriage, but it is not a biblical requirement, and we want to be careful that we don't make it into that. "But in vain they do worship me, teaching *for* doctrines the commandments of men" (Matthew 15:9). Support your son, and continue to encourage him to follow his Lord.

What If He Misspent His Money?

Start now! If your son has already spent the income he has earned, that can't change. Solomon said, "The thing that hath been, it *is that* which shall be; and that which is done is that which shall be done: and *there is* no new *thing* under the sun" (Ecclesiastes 1:9). How many of us made mistakes like that?

It may be that your son won't recover and be able to buy his house debt-free. Your job, however, is to encourage him to try. Often the best way to get out of a problem is to avoid it in the first place. When that isn't possible, though, we learn from past mistakes and purpose not to repeat them. It may be that your son will have to settle for less of a house than he would have been able to buy had he been saving his finances from the start, but it is a great learning opportunity for him.

If you have more children following, they can learn from this son's example. Purpose to discover any errors you made with your first son so you can avoid them with your remaining children. The problem will usually involve appetites for things that consume their money. As parents, you can continue to work with your sons to move them away from frivolous spending and toward saving.

If your son doesn't change, however, things will probably only get worse. Once he has a family of his own, he will have more bills and less money. If he continues to spend unnecessarily, he will likely experience marriage problems in addition to financial pressures. Be determined to help him toward the spiritual growth necessary in his life to reverse the spending mentality or the lack of motivation to learn skills and work.

What If My Son Doesn't Make Much Money?

Start now! There are several options if your son doesn't make much money. The first and most important is that he be ultra careful not to spend what he does earn. Remember the table in chapter 6 showing the impact of spending on one's ability to save? Even if he made $10 an hour, he could save $100,000 in under nine years. If he started saving when he was 18, he would achieve his goal when he was 26.

Perhaps your son will set his sights on an older, smaller home that may cost significantly less than other homes. In our town, many such homes are available for around $50,000. They make great starter homes. That would only take him 4.3 years to save for.

Even then, however, $10 an hour would be a very difficult wage on which to raise a family. So during those years of working and saving, he would have had time to learn new skills. He should do this for the good of his future family. There is every likelihood that when your son is 25, he could be making $25 or more an hour. With his house paid for, he could nicely support a family with that wage.

Your son can also cry out to the Lord for creative solutions for a debt-free house. "… The effectual fervent prayer of a righteous man availeth much" (James 5:16). Remember Jacob and how he acquired his debt-free house by clearing the land at the old pallet factory? Ben built a house with his dad and multiplied his savings when he sold it. He had enough money to build his house debt-free after that. Bill earned a very low wage, and yet God led him to a house that was purchased for the least cost of all the examples we have shared.

We get excited when we see God respond to hard-working young men who have the goal of being debt-free. There are so many different situations, but God is always there working behind the scenes.

What If He Wants to Go to College First?

As we have already indicated, going to college can be a great hindrance to buying a house debt-free. It's interesting because college is generally seen as the prerequisite for debt-free living, but sadly, it often doesn't seem to be the financial windfall that was hoped for. Most come out of college and quickly enter into living in debt through credit cards, auto loans, and home mortgages. We have already shared the ways that college hinders buying a house debt-free. Remember that college is costly, regularly requires debt to complete, takes four to six prime income-producing years out of a person's life, and exposes our children to ungodly influences. When our sons begin their own businesses or work for someone during those college years, they avoid those obstacles to a debt-free house.

While going to college can be a big hindrance to purchasing a house debt-free, it doesn't make it impossible. Andrew financed his own way through college with his savings, a $12,000 loan from his dad, and working as an intern at the company that eventually hired him. He lived at home while going to college, which kept his expenses minimal. When he graduated, he had $300 to his name.

Over the next four years, he continued to live at home, work, and save for a house. When he attempted to repay his dad for the loan, his dad declined the payment.

Andrew had saved over $100,000 and was ready to purchase a house. He evaluated his three possible housing options: (1) buy a reasonably modest house that was occupancy ready; (2) buy a fixer-upper and pay a contractor to update it; or (3) buy a fixer-upper and do the work himself. At age 26, Andrew purchased a fixer-upper home debt-free for $70,000, planning to do the work himself. He had $30,000 available for his remodel and still had an "emergency" fund in savings. He is now working on the renovations. Andrew managed college and a debt-free house before he was 30, but he is a rarity. Often a young man finds the woman of his dreams while at college and gets married soon after. Then he has the added financial responsibilities that go with a family that make it very difficult to save for a debt-free house.

We would suggest that if college is what your son believes is necessary for his future he plan to first work long enough to save for his house. Then go to college after doing so. Remember that distance learning is preferable while living at home, keeping expenses down and mitigating some of the negative influences of college life. It might be that in the interim, the Lord will establish your son in a business or a job where he realizes a college degree isn't necessary for what the Lord wants to do with his life. If he does end up going to college, he will have his "nest egg" available for his house should the Lord be directing him to marriage after college.

What If His Goal is $500,000?

Start now! Your son certainly won't make a goal of $500,000 if he doesn't aggressively begin right away earning and saving money. For this book, we are assuming a savings of $100,000–$200,000 for a starter home. Obviously a $500,000 house is a much more lofty goal.

You might first discuss with your son why he feels he needs $500,000 for a home. Is that what starter homes in your area cost, or is there a level of covetousness in his heart?

You can work together to discover what it will take financially to have $500,000 in the bank. To accomplish that, one must save for a long time or earn a very handsome hourly wage. It would take someone making $25 an hour 8.5 years to save $250,000, if he spent only $50 per week. Your son would need to make $50 an hour for the same length of time to achieve his goal of $500,000.

That isn't totally impossible. Many businesses charge over $50 per hour for their services; however, they have overhead and profit built in. If your son owns his business and works from home, overhead is low, and the profit belongs to him. Often computer-related activities bill over $75 an hour and even fees over $100 an hour are not uncommon. Automotive shops charge $60–$70 per hour. Your son will need to gain skills and start a business that will net these kinds of wages if his goal is $500,000.

Probably for this "what if," it is best to give your son a realistic picture of what it takes to earn and save that amount of money. You could encourage him toward a goal of $200,000 and then to re-evaluate where he is in life to see if any circumstances or direction from the Lord have changed when that goal is met.

What If We Are Not Debt-Free?

Start now! When parents are not debt-free themselves, they may feel it is hypocritical to encourage their sons toward a goal of debt-free living and purchasing homes debt-free. We were still in debt when we began setting a debt-free vision in front of our children, but we had grasped the goal of becoming a debt-free family.

If you are in bondage to debt, you can determine right now to take steps to be free of it. Then you will not only be moving in the debt-free direction but also be setting an example for your children. Begin with paying off high-interest credit card debt, then auto loans, and finally work on your mortgage. We think your family will celebrate with each debt that is paid off.

When you talk about the blessing of being debt-free and the bondage of debt with your children, you will help them avoid those same problems. Working as a family toward being more frugal and putting any extra funds possible toward debt payoff draws the family together. You are working as a team toward a common goal. Your motivation for a debt-free family will be motivation for your children, too.

What If He Fails?

What exactly would constitute failure? Is it your son's not reaching his financial goal for a debt-free house? Wouldn't it be better, though, to aim for the goal than not to try in the first place? Most likely he would have some measure of success and perhaps much success. We would rather our sons have 90% or even 50% of what they would need for a debt-free house than to have nothing at all.

Perhaps failure is starting a business but not having it flourish so that your son's savings don't accumulate as he envisioned. Joseph told Steve about an article he read concerning a startup business owner. His current successful endeavor was the second-fastest growing business in his state. That's why he was being interviewed! The amazing part of the story, though, was that he had tried nine previous businesses that had all failed. What if he had given up after the first nine attempts?

One wise business owner Steve knew said he learned much more from his proposals that didn't win the contract than those that did. If your son's business fails, he learns what went wrong and what to do better next time. He doesn't want to live in the past but in the new day. He doesn't give up but rather picks himself up and tries again.

The only failure we see is the failure not to grasp the goal, not to work toward it, and not to continue when obstacles arise—the failure to be committed. What we are encouraging your sons toward isn't "name it, claim it" or simply positive thinking. It is about following the Lord Jesus through initiative, determination, and hard work. "I can do all things through Christ which strengtheneth me" (Philippians 4:13). Even the world understands how important one's commitment is to achieving goals. Henry Ford said, "If you believe you can do a thing, or believe you can't do a thing, you are right."

Fear of failure is the reason some have not accomplished great things. Most people have at least a few superb ideas with potential, but few act on them because they are afraid it might not work. That is certainly not a good reason to quit before starting. "For God hath not given us the spirit of fear; but of power, and of love, and of a sound mind" (2 Timothy 1:7). Set aside thoughts of failure and encourage your son to own the goal and strive toward it.

Overcome the "What Ifs"

We think there is a simple solution to most of the "what ifs" presented here and others that might come up. You already know the solution. It is to ignore the "what ifs" and start the process of working and saving toward a debt-free house. Then see what the Lord does and where He takes your son. Anything he has saved will be better than nothing at all.

With prayer, persistence, diligence, frugality, patience, and contentment, however, exciting outcomes come when one has a goal of a debt-free-house. You have seen it in the stories of the young men in these chapters. They are young men just like your son. Had they listened to and given in to the "what ifs," most likely they would not currently own their homes debt-free. Help your son past any "what ifs" he brings up so he can have a debt-free house testimony to God's glory.

Chapter 14

- What are your son's "what ifs"?
- How can you help him past them?

15 LIVE THE VISION

Joseph, our third son, began learning to program computers when he was 10 years old. We wanted to direct him to activities that would be productive with his time. We provided him with a book so he could learn Delphi, which was an object-oriented Pascal language, and a refurbished HP computer to use. Within four years of part-time study, his skills were such that he was able to take on some significant programming jobs for others that paid him $25 an hour. He was still in school so he couldn't work full-time, but he was able to save a decent amount because of his high wages.

When Joseph graduated from high school, he and his younger brother John volunteered to build a new family home. You have already heard part of that story when we told about

Christopher's buying our house. At that time, Joseph and John said they would build the house so Steve could primarily continue ministering and writing. It took three years with a great deal of family effort to build the house. During those years, Joseph had very little income-producing time.

While building the house, Joseph and John decided that they would like to start a remodeling business together. They did that for one year. Travel with our family ministry, however, meant a significant number of weeks each year when they wouldn't be able to earn construction income. In addition, most customers would not want to wait four to six weeks for their project while the boys were away. Joseph realized that he could take his programming work on the road with us; plus he made a much higher hourly rate from programming than remodeling.

At 20, Joseph began contract programming with a billable hourly rate of $60. By the time he was 23, he had saved over $100,000 and began looking for a house. We already mentioned that the house he purchased had been on the market for a year, taken off for an extended period of time, and then re-listed for a lower price of $90,000. Joseph saw it come up right away and asked to see it. The house was in serious need of updating, but it would have been livable if necessary. Joseph had cash to pay, and he made a low offer. Because the house was part of an estate, the seller's agent encouraged the heirs to accept the cash offer of $71,000 to get the estate settled quickly.

With Joseph's building experience, he was planning to invest more of his savings plus his time to fix up the house. Because of the good purchase price he got, he had funds left for the remodel. Joseph's building skills are helping him with the house he now owns. Even though he isn't using them to produce income, he is saving money by doing the work on his home himself. Remember every dollar saved is up to a $1.50 earned. If in the future his computer work dries up, he can fall back on his construction experience.

Adult children who are walking faithfully with the Lord Jesus are a parent's greatest delight. "I have no greater joy than to hear that my children walk in truth" (3 John 1:4). Having sons achieve their goal of being debt-free is also pretty nice. Some young men will achieve this goal on their own, but for most their parent's example, instruction, and encouragement will be key. Will you come alongside your son?

Debt's Bondage

In general a mortgage is seen as the only way to purchase a home. Many haven't been challenged to think they could buy a house debt-free, and this is especially true for younger people. Life experience and Scripture tell us of the bondage and pressure debt can bring into our lives.

"And there was a great cry of the people and of their wives against their brethren the Jews. For there were that said, We, our sons, and our daughters, *are* many: therefore we take up corn *for them*, that we may eat, and live. *Some* also there were that said,

We have mortgaged our lands, vineyards, and houses, that we might buy corn, because of the dearth. There were also that said, We have borrowed money for the king's tribute, *and that upon* our lands and vineyards. Yet now our flesh *is* as the flesh of our brethren, our children as their children: and, lo, we bring into bondage our sons and our daughters to be servants, and *some* of our daughters are brought unto bondage *already*: neither *is it* in our power *to redeem them*; for other men have our lands and vineyards" (Nehemiah 5:1-5).

While we might enjoy what our debt allows us to have, if we ever come to a place of not being able to make the promised payments on the loan and face losing whatever our debt procured for us, the stress is severe.

The time to set before our sons the possibility and goal of buying a house debt-free is while they are still living with us at home. We can save them the money lost in interest and the sleepless nights if payments can't be made and help them lay a solid financial foundation by directing them to want a debt-free house and lifestyle.

Determination

Through the years, we have heard many parents say their son couldn't buy a house debt-free because of x, y, or z. Admittedly, some of their "reasons" have merit why it would be difficult, but we can't remember hearing anything that was a reason why he shouldn't try.

We wonder if the real reason might be they lack the will to tackle something that sounds difficult. Instead of that mindset, what about seeing challenges as good for us? We suppose that is one reason our family has enjoyed climbing fourteeners in Colorado. We like a challenge. Every time we have set out to climb a fourteener, no one in our family knows for sure he will make it, but each is determined to give it all they have.

One year Joseph developed severe knee pain and Jesse's foot began hurting him greatly. Steve, Teri, and the girls have on different climbs developed altitude sickness. Despite those hardships, however, each one successfully continued to hike. In climbs and life, different things can happen to derail us from our goals. We don't let that stop us from being committed to giving it all we can to accomplish the task at hand.

Aren't we inspired reading about the conquests of David's mighty men? What isn't recorded in Scripture is the rigorous conditioning they went through, the long hours of practice, the injuries they sustained, and their many less-notable battles that prepared them to be mighty men.

Thankfully, we don't have those kinds of battles to buy a house debt-free, yet buying a house will entail diligence, hard work, a long time, and perhaps even setbacks. Being debt-free is an area, though, where a son can accomplish something on a grand scale. There are so few men today who have the discipline and determination to achieve this goal. It isn't so a son can say, "Look at what I did," but so he can say, "Look at what my God did. God is so faithful!"

Sacrifice

Generally, any significant accomplishment involves a background of sacrifice and effort. This typifies all that parents do in raising mighty sons of virtue and character who depend on the Lord Jesus. You will have almost as much a part of your son's debt-free house as he does.

Parents give the vision, and they model the lifestyle for their children. If you aren't debt-free now, you can set that goal for yourself and start working toward it, while encouraging your son in the same direction.

Situations will arise when you will provide guidance to your son. The priority he places on saving and buying a house debt-free will be challenged, and his ultimate success will depend on how his priorities are managed. There will be a host of fun and expensive things that come along. Will he stay true to his goal or be pulled off course? You will be important in this process, and your commitment to encourage him will likely be tested.

As he grows older, your position of authority in his life will migrate to one of counselor. You may not be able to buy a house for him, but you are certainly capable of cheering him on to success. You can teach him to seek the Lord and rely fully on Him. "If any of you lack wisdom, let him ask of God, that giveth to all *men* liberally, and upbraideth not; and it shall be given him" (James 1:5).

The Nehemiah Example

History is full of naysayers who have attempted to dissuade those committed to following a direction the Lord has given to them. Nehemiah faced similar opposition.

"But it came to pass, that when Sanballat heard that we builded the wall, he was wroth, and took great indignation, and mocked the Jews. And he spake before his brethren and the army of Samaria, and said, What do these feeble Jews? will they fortify themselves? will they sacrifice? will they make an end in a day? will they revive the stones out of the heaps of the rubbish which are burned?" (Nehemiah 4:1-2). Sanballat was the governor of Samaria, and he was upset that Jerusalem was being rebuilt. He put great pressure on Nehemiah to stop. Martin Luther said, "Faith is a living, daring confidence in God's grace." It took faith and courage for Nehemiah and his men to build in the face of opposition.

Nehemiah's opposition grew stronger. "And conspired all of them together to come *and* to fight against Jerusalem, and to hinder it" (Nehemiah 4:8). Words were not enough. The opposition was now planning to use force. What did Nehemiah do? Did he give up because of the threats and conspiracy? We then read, "Nevertheless we made our prayer unto our God, and set a watch against them day and night, because of them" (Nehemiah 4:9). Nehemiah wasn't afraid or dismayed by the naysayers' threats. He turned to the Lord in prayer, and so must we. Next we read that they followed their prayer with action.

It is a good thing to instill in our children the desire for debt-free lives and even better to help them along that path. Rebuilding the walls of Jerusalem seemed like an almost impossible job. The destruction was so great that not one stone remained upon another. Yet they believed in their mission and that God would enable them.

It will take faith and courage for you to inspire your sons to forsake the easy way of the world, not get a mortgage, and be debt-free. You will not have such a historical opportunity to rebuild the walls as Nehemiah did to God's glory, but you can instill in your children the high goal of living debt-free and give them the determination to continue toward that goal despite opposition.

The Challenge

Young men who will take on the debt-free challenge are young men who are willing to learn new skills and work hard. They will seek the Lord Jesus for direction in their lives, and they will set aside temporary pleasures for future benefits.

Attaining the goal of buying his house debt-free may be the biggest challenge your son has faced so far in his life. Might some not make it? Possibly, but we must remain committed to our belief that the goal is attainable and encourage them all along the way. "And he said unto me, My grace is sufficient for thee: for my strength is made perfect in weakness. Most gladly therefore will I rather glory in my infirmities, that the power of Christ may rest upon me. Therefore I take pleasure in infirmities, in reproaches, in necessities, in persecutions, in distresses for Christ's sake: for when I am weak, then am I strong" (2 Corinthians 12:9-10).

The challenges that pose a hindrance to his buying a home debt-free are nothing but opportunities for God to show Himself strong! We think your son will be better having set out for the goal, even if he doesn't make it, than to say "it is too hard" and not start.

In Perspective

Please keep in mind that living debt-free is not a Scriptural mandate. Some Scripture passages certainly indicate the negative aspects of debt and possible consequences of it, but we don't want to imply that the Bible says outright that debt is sin.

We are trying to present an exciting possibility for a different way of life financially than what the world typically suggests. We see Scripture endorsing this approach as well when it speaks negatively of borrowing, positively of lending, and says that the borrower is servant to the lender. We do not, however, want to take Scripture further than what it says and put man-imposed burdens on our children in the name of being spiritual.

More Encouragement

We suggest that you get a copy of *Buying a House Debt-Free* for each of your sons. Write a note in it expressing your vision for him to own his home debt-free. Read *Buying a House Debt-Free* with your children. Why not give a copy to each set of grandparents to get their endorsement of this direction for your sons? Your son needs encouragement, and the more people who are cheering him on, the better! Also think about when someone gives you a book versus loans it to you. It conveys, "You are important enough to give this gift to you," and it communicates an added measure of value on what you are giving. The more support you can get, the better!

A Family with a Vision

We are a family just like yours. When we gave our sons the vision of owning homes debt-free, it seemed impossible. Yet we have watched three of our sons develop skills, work hard, save their money, and then purchase their homes debt-free—and our two younger sons are close behind them. It wasn't impossible, but it would have been if they had never owned the vision or started toward the goal.

We have shared stories of other young men who have debt-free homes to inspire and challenge you to the possibilities for your sons. You can read this material and set it down saying, "It is too hard." Your sons will be the losers. On the other hand, you can read this material, set it down, and say, "We can do it!" Your sons will be the winners.

We know that not everyone will receive this information. Many will read it and think it is too difficult. They won't even take steps to try. We hope and pray that you aren't one of those parents. Remember, the question isn't, "Is it possible for him to buy his house debt-free?" but rather, "Will he commit to start toward the goal?" We would like you to be the parents who set the vision for their sons (and daughters) who want to break out of the rut and who head down the path that will enable those young men to own their homes debt-free.

Begin now, whether your son is five or twenty. We know families whose little boys, ages five and six, are saving to buy their houses debt-free. Even if your son is older, it isn't too late. He will benefit from grabbing the vision of a debt-free house and moving toward that end.

We hope you embrace the vision—and not only embrace it but also work toward helping your son fulfill it. Then, when your son has a house debt-free, you will realize that it was possible. Your son has done what others said was impossible. He owns a debt-free home and isn't even 30-years-old!

Chapter 15 Questions

- What specific steps will you take to start your son toward a debt-free house?
- How will these steps be implemented?

- Who are you going to give *Buying a House Debt-Free* that might encourage your son?
- Who are the naysayers who would benefit from *Buying a House Debt-Free* to whom you could give it?

RESOURCES

REDEEMING THE TIME

A Practical Guide to a Christian Man's Time Management

by Steven Maxwell

- Works for men with any kind of job.
- Addresses time robbers.
- Teaches how to properly balance everything.
- Includes concrete, step-by-step help.
- Has testimonies from other dads.
- Available in paperback or unabridged audiobook.

"It is a wonderful book. It has really changed my life. I've got more time than I ever thought I would have." Jeff

"After reading this book, I have a better idea and understanding of what God expects from me as the DAD!" Lane

Available at Titus2.com

RESOURCES

PREPARING SONS

to Provide for a Single-Income Family

by Steven Maxwell

- Written by Steve, dad to five sons.
- Contains practical suggestions.
- Equips parents to have a purpose/plan.
- Begins with preschool and finishes with adulthood.
- Gives solid information on raising sons.
- Available in paperback or unabridged audiobook.

"You are dealing with topics that no one I know of has dealt with as thoroughly and practically as you have." Dr. S.M. Davis

"Preparing Sons was a big blessing to my husband. All you ladies should get a copy for your husband and every church library needs one." Shelly

Available at Titus2.com

MAKING GREAT CONVERSA-TIONALISTS

by Steven & Teri Maxwell

- Does your child give one-word answers?
- Do you have one of those "shy" children?
- Does your child only know how to talk about himself?
- What does it take to make a worthwhile conversation?
- Learn how to equip your children to become great conversationalists!

"This book should be required reading material for every parent of a school-aged child in America!" Henry

"Our children grew in conversation boldness and ability." Jessica

Available at Titus2.com

RESOURCES

KEEPING OUR CHILDREN'S HEARTS

Our Vital Priority

by Steven and Teri Maxwell

- Covers the crucial area of children's hearts.
- Has true-life examples/experience from Maxwells'.
- Shares how to avoid teen rebellion.
- Defines key factors that influence children's hearts.
- Addresses goal setting for your family.
- Refutes naysayers.

"The most complete and most balanced book I have read on how to raise children who won't rebel!" Dr. S. M. Davis

"It truly is my top child rearing book now. You have brought together all the issues we have been striving to understand and achievements we hope to make with our children." Kathryn

Available at Titus2.com

MANAGERS OF THEIR HOMES

A Practical Guide to Daily Scheduling for Christian Homeschool Families

by Steven and Teri Maxwell

- Works for families of all sizes.
- Leads in making a schedule.
- Includes hands-on Scheduling Kit.
- Filled with practical suggestions.
- Teaches how to schedule children's time.
- Contains a chapter for dads by Steve.
- Has thirty real-life example schedules.

"My schedule has given me back my sanity!! I can't believe the way my life has changed since implementing a schedule." Tracy

"I had read almost every organizational book there was, and I still couldn't get to where I wanted to be until I applied this method!" Corrie

Available at Titus2.com

MANAGERS OF THEIR CHORES

A Practical Guide to Children's Chores

by Steven and Teri Maxwell

- Instructs in developing your chore system.
- Includes ChorePacks and supplies for four children.
- Equips parents to implement a chore system.
- Works for families of all sizes.
- Contains a chapter for dads by Steve.
- Has many helpful example chore systems.
- Allows picture chorecards to be made online.

"I can't believe how much time we have gained in our days now that we have our ChorePack system in place." Kendra

"Its simplicity and ease of use encouraged independence and accountability at a young age." Rachel

Available at Titus2.com

MANAGERS OF THEIR SCHOOLS

A Practical Guide to Homeschooling

by Steven and Teri Maxwell

- Written by long-time homeschool parents of eight.
- Includes practical advice for curriculum decisions.
- Shares homeschool methods that have worked.
- Contains a chapter for dads by Steve.
- Has helpful information on managing math.
- Teaches how to effectively manage your homeschool.
- Discount section in the back.

"I have learned so much from the book. The time I will save in planning for this school year is astronomical!" Jessica

"The book was well-written and thought provoking, with good use of examples to make it come alive and see how it could work for me." Sandy

Available at Titus2.com

RESOURCES

SWEET JOURNEY

A Bible Study

by Teri Maxwell

- Contains potential to transform a life.
- Covers crucial spiritual foundations.
- Gives direction to solutions to problems.
- Has how-tos for a close walk with Jesus.
- Includes study questions
- Is in Bible study format.

"This book is a treasure that will lead you on to the BEST TREASURE of all—a 'sweet journey' with Him." Michelle

"Anyone who will read this book will feel like they've just taken the hand of a dear friend and been led step by step in a journey to finding out how to draw closer to Jesus Christ." Susi

Available at Titus2.com

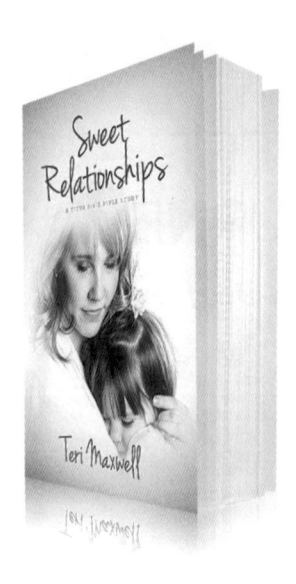

SWEET RELATIONSHIPS

A Bible Study

by Teri Maxwell

- Guides in deepening precious relationships.
- Contains helpful how-tos and ideas.
- Perfect for individual or mother/daughter study.
- Includes study questions.
- Is in Bible study format.

"*Sweet Relationships* has been a huge benefit in my life. I needed each chapter. It is such an encouragement to me as a stay at home wife and homeschooling mom." Kara

"Teri, what richness within those pages. God is using it in so many ways in my life. There is a pureness and a sweetness in just doing the study, that I desire it to change my heart and overflow in the relationships so very dear to me." Joy

Available at Titus2.com

RESOURCES

HOMESCHOOLING WITH A MEEK AND QUIET SPIRIT

by Teri Maxwell

- Tried-and-true personal experience from Teri.
- Delves into heart issues.
- Gives moms hope for change.
- Addresses worry, anger, and depression.
- Includes projects.

"This is one of the best, most helpful, encouraging, and empathetic books I've read during my 5 years of homeschooling." Cassandra

"I wish all moms, regardless of their school choice, could read Homeschooling with a Meek and Quiet Spirit.*"* Kathy

"It is not just for homeschooling moms, but any mom who wants to be the best mom she can be. It was challenging, enlightening, and encouraging." Jennifer

Available at Titus2.com

THE MOODY FAMILY SERIES

by Sarah Maxwell

- Fictional series/based on true life.
- Contains positive role models for children.
- Includes every day adventures.
- Homeschool family are main characters.
- Readers identify with the family.
- Popular with children of all ages.

"My six-year-old son asked Jesus into his heart while we were reading *Autumn with the Moodys*. These books are wonderful, heart-warming Christian reading." Rebecca

"At last, a Christian book series that is engaging and encourages my children to love Jesus more and bless their family and friends." Karen

Available at Titus2.com

RESOURCES

JUST AROUND THE CORNER

Encouragement and Challenge for Christian Dads and Moms

Volumes 1 and 2

by Steven and Teri Maxwell

- Challenge and encouragement in short articles.
- Much-needed guidance for dads.
- Indexed to easily find topics.
- Deals with parenting, husband/wife relationships, and more.

"*Just Around the Corner has helped me to regain my focus and carry on to what God has called me to do.*" Michelle

Available at Titus2.com

FEED MY SHEEP

A Practical Guide to Daily Family Bible Time
2 CD Album

by Steve Maxwell

- Tried and failed family devotions?
- Here's how to have family Bible time—guaranteed!

ENCOURAGE-MENT FOR THE HOMESCHOOL FAMILY

10 CD Album

by Steve & Teri Maxwell

- Nine-session audio seminar on ten CDs.
- Sessions will encourage, exhort, and equip families.
- Value-priced album!

Available at Titus2.com